Sleep in Me

American Lives

Series editor: Tobias Wolff

University of Nebraska Press | Lincoln and London

Sleep in Me
Jon Pineda

All rights reserved
Manufactured in the
United States of America
⊚
Library of Congress
Cataloging-in-Publication Data
Pineda, Jon, 1971–
Sleep in me / Jon Pineda.
p.   cm. — (American lives)
ISBN 978-0-8032-2535-0 (cloth : alk. paper)
1. Pineda, Jon, 1971– — Childhood and youth.
2. Pineda, Jon, 1971– — Family. 3. Authors,
American — 21st century — Biography.
4. Filipino Americans — Biography.
5. Filipino American families. 6. Brothers
and sisters — United States. 7. Sisters —
United States — Biography. 8. Traffic
accident victims — United States — Biography. 9. Great Bridge (Chesapeake, Va.) —
Biography. I. Title.
PS3616.I565Z46   2010
811'.6 — dc22
[B]
2010001661

Set in Arno Pro by Bob Reitz.

for Amy, *my secret weapon*

And yet barely a girl, and leaping
out of this happy harmony of song and lyre,
and shining clearly through her veils of Spring,
and made herself a bed inside my ear.

And slept in me. And her sleep was all.

Rilke, "The Sonnets to Orpheus"

Contents

Acknowledgments

My wife, Amy, read and edited every version. Her immense patience for this manuscript was rivaled only by the invaluable insight she offered. I'm grateful to my family for sharing with me their memories of Rica, and equally grateful to my friends for their encouragement and support. Works by Greg Bottoms, Claudia Emerson, James Hoch, and Nick Montemarano were especially influential.

I'm indebted to Jim McKean, an amazing teacher and a generous soul. His guidance helped me as I began the initial draft of the manuscript. To my colleagues and students in the MFA program at Queens University of Charlotte, you never cease to inspire. *Viva Fred Leebron! Viva Mike Kobre!*

My sincerest thanks to Ladette Randolph, Kristen Elias Rowley, and the staff at the University of Nebraska Press for making this book happen. Laurie Alberts and Jennifer Brice provided amazing advice for the final revision as well.

Several chapters first appeared (under the title "Learning the Language") in the literary journal *Gulf Coast*. A thousand thanks to the editors.

I wish to express my deepest gratitude to John Moore and his family.

I.

Learning the Language

Because we were boys, not yet teenagers, we would laugh to ourselves when we said words like *fuck* or *cocksucker* or *cunt*. We would
gather what little bit of money we could find around our houses,
usually in the sticky folds of couches, and walk up to the gas station
on Battlefield Boulevard. People filling their cars before heading
into Great Bridge would stare at us like we were strays. You could
tell by their pursed lips. They were hoping we wouldn't wander any
farther than where we were. Our hair tousled, our shirts stretched,
brushed with grass stains and some blood garnered from a neighborhood football game. Each of us was a pariah-in-training.

Sometimes, emboldened, we'd stare back in disgust or yell
things and flip them off. It was all part of the role. They expected
it of us. At the pay counter, we'd smirk at the receding hairline of
the clerk, an old speckled man with palsy who would rather read
his paper than have to look his customers in the eye. We blessed
this apathy. Word had gotten around too. His inattention couldn't
have been better. While towers of coins tumbled into his shaky
hand, we'd demand soft packs of Marlboro or Camel or Kool brand
cigarettes. Without so much as glancing at us, he'd smile.

Sometimes we only wanted the finger-sized, cherry-flavored
cigars with crimped tips, the ones kept arranged in a container
near the register. They would be next to the single roses wrapped
in plastic tubes, vials of green water cupping the clipped stems. In

triumph we bore our stash back to the fort, a rusted maintenance van that had been left to rot in a side lot near Timmy's house. Even in warm months, we'd sit inside this van. The doors and windows would be sealed shut, and we'd thumb slowly through issues of *Penthouse* or *Hustler* someone's uncle had given us.

I remember in one there was a woman whose body had been decorated to resemble a landscape. Tiny orange diamond-shaped construction signs balanced on her nipples while Matchbox cars of all sizes lined up in a traffic jam between her breasts. Other cars heading south on the makeshift road of her belly actually disappeared inside her. In another issue some of the pages would be torn. More often than not there would be a worn oval section between a woman's legs. Of course we knew what from, and on subsequent pages, there were places where the heads of these naked women should be but weren't. The images beyond violated, but we didn't care. We didn't really think of them as being violated, didn't know the various forms violations could take.

Instead, we'd cough and laugh as we spoke in what we thought was the language of men. We were learning the language. We wanted to become men so badly we'd do whatever we thought was necessary. Break all the rules, if that's what it took. It didn't matter that we had kissed girls already. Or had felt a few up. Everyone had. The van became a sanctum where any knowledge gleaned from the adult world was shared with all. In a full sweat, we'd throw out questions to each other, ask if any of us knew what certain girls from our school would really do. One of us would inevitably offer a story about so-and-so doing this and that with so-and-so. I would listen intently, as would the others.

Once, someone put two fingers in the air, the fingers close together like their knuckles were knees to a pair of modest legs. He said, You want to smell what it smells like?

We were nervous, said *Fuck*, no, but then each took a turn.

Who is it? I said, stepping back, feeling like I had to sneeze.

You don't know? he said, laughing.

Who is it? I said.

Man, it's just your sister, he said.

Of course I knew it wasn't, but I charged at him anyway. You had to do that. It's what boys did. We fell to the floor, and he was laughing, saying he was just kidding, just kidding for fuck's sake. Soon, all of us were laughing. It was how it was. We were mostly friends, easily forgiven for whatever lines we crossed with one another.

Sorry, he said. I didn't mean your sister.

He brushed dust from his shirt as he stood up. He smiled. It was the kind when people only barely show you their teeth. Gums with just a trace of teeth. Like they have something in their mouth they don't want to let out just yet.

Don't say it, I said. I knew what was coming.

What? he said. Like your mom cares if I tell you.

That's it, I said, and we were down on the floor of the van again.

Beneath the Surface

Before my sister Rica's accident, I thought I might stay a boy forever. If I wasn't roasting inside that abandoned van, scheming under sheets of smoke, I was spending days after school roaming with other boys from the neighborhood. Boys whose names when I think of them now are only ghosts in a far off landscape — Heath, Timothy, Glen. There was even one whose last name was Hill.

Along the rear of Hill's house ran a creek where a part of the land ended and formed a small promise of open water. There we would not hesitate to shoot at the heads of cottonmouths. We'd use .22s instead of Hill's father's 12- or 20-gauge shotguns. We thought we were being responsible by forgoing the larger guns, especially since our antics were done usually from the safety of the dock nearby.

The dock's crinoline tin roof would also shield us from the sun casting long jagged-edged shadows. If we thought about it, we could picture someone holding a giant handsaw above us, a hint of some invisible but imminent danger. If we weren't shooting at something, we were oddly pensive. We'd cast lines through the clouded water and wait for the first bite from anything. *Fish, snake, snapping turtle.* It didn't matter. We wished only for what lived beneath the surface.

One day, on our way down to the creek, we stopped first for ammunition. We crouched in front of Hill's house, where the edge of pavement seemed to unravel at the end of Snowberry Lane.

Above us ragged squirrels were nervous in the clustered oaks and maples. They jumped from branch to branch and scurried spirals up and down the wrinkled trunks.

These trees marked the beginning of a haze every boy in the neighborhood disappeared within. Huddled, like cavemen around a ring of stones nursing a fire through their whispering, we pulled at each black chunk of tarmac still sticky, giving off a blunt sucking sound. Pieces wrenched free were the size of huge brownies, slowly folding in our hands from the heat. In water they hardened into caustic polygons. They became the primitive tools we lugged in buckets down to the creek.

Low tide was that odd time of day when the murkiness receded and left gray moss-covered banks dimpled with mud and the random blemish of a coiled snake. After the water had seemingly drained into the scattered pools, we would gather up our buckets and head in the direction of uncharted marsh. In our other hands were the enormous pieces of pavement. We'd sling them into puddles and wait for the bait.

The force of each impact would thrust silvered minnows onto the banks to flail, and we'd walk around them, examining them as they bounced and spun like a handful of BB's released onto a tiled floor. We'd miss some entirely. Others we'd momentarily hold only to have them glide through our fingers. Sometimes we'd end up clutching mud, groping some, and then lucky, we'd slip the bodies into the buckets, where we kept a little water for the other minnows. It wasn't much water, just enough to keep them alive.

Later, we'd return to the dock with our catch and wait for high tide. With high tide came the monstrous catfish, those bloated and slimy submarines, whiskered and nearly blind. They looked to us to be from another planet. Being boys hinged to this small space of earth, we wanted to do our part. We craved to torture them in the grass.

Then we did.

An Almost Perfect Circle

The only sound around us was the creaking swing of each handle. Our buckets were like pendulums. We stepped slowly off the dock and into the creek bed. They would sway and keep time while our footsteps sank half an inch at the very least into the slimy muck. Years before, I had jumped off this same dock barefoot, barely making a splash and sinking straight down.

That's when I felt a slight pinch.

Surfacing, I found an apron of blood tied to the water around me. I had come down heel first onto a piece of glass. I nearly lost that part of my foot. What made it worse was that I had already been grounded by my mother and wasn't supposed to have left the house at all. It didn't take cutting my foot to learn dangerous things lived in this water, it was simply reinforcement.

Now with low tide exposing the creek bed, I followed the others. We could have been walking on slugs, the bubbling gunk squishing between our toes. It was farther down that our crew of boys found lots of puddles to disturb. We threw the pavement chunks, and the minnows suddenly appeared in the glory of individual struggles. There were big ones and barely visible ones. Whatever size, it didn't matter. We gathered them all and pushed forward, around several more bends and under the curved branches of trees lining the creek.

It turns out we had gone farther on foot than we ever had, past our normal stopping point, all the way to the view where the creek opened onto hundreds of miniature islands buffered with cord grass. I thought then of pictures my father had shown me, those of his homeland, the Philippines. An archipelago nebulous in my mind's eye, with its thousands of islands, where I was convinced even the crickets (if they existed there, I didn't really know) must have spoken different dialects.

I had never met any of my relatives. In so many ways our father was the sole ambassador to a country of his own making. Aside from tales of Filipino vampires, he had told me stories of snakes they had found in the countryside. The snakes were massive things of flesh and muscle that surprised and even threatened villagers before the giant serpents were inevitably caught and stripped of their lives and thrown over a spit and eaten by all.

Though I don't know if it was my father's intent, I was mesmerized by the actions of those villagers. They didn't seem brutal, but rather necessary. My father had come from a place where it seemed a life was nothing more than a series of risks, and with those risks were earned celebrations. I had to remember this—somewhere in my blood was my father's blood, his blood nourished by the snakes of a memory, a justified undoing.

The tide had started its way back. It was quiet. Its sinuous quality could make the hair on the back of my neck stand up if I thought too long about it. Our steps began now with small splashes but sank down farther than before. We should head back, Hill said. We nodded, but still gazed at the marsh and the half-light that was leaving us or me, at least, feeling moved. By what, I couldn't really say.

Perhaps it was the cloistering atmosphere of the creek. It had opened up to where it all felt vast. I don't know. I was just eleven and had only really known loss through my father's naval deployments overseas.

Glen, the oldest of our group, had spotted it. Before the rest of us followed the length of his gawky arm, he already had his sights on the moccasin. Then we saw it for ourselves. It rested upon an embankment. It was a deadly swirl of brown and black capped with a white, pinkish mouth. The mouth lay unhinged and open. Looking in shape and texture like petals of some exotic tropical flower you should never touch, or even smell for that matter.

There, Glen said, stepping toward the moccasin. He was still pointing.

We each must have eyed at the same time the deadly beauty of it, because it lured us closer. We were hypnotized, drawn slowly into the sphere of its lunging reach. Because we were boys and nearly fearless, our one mind drew each arm back and let out a breath that became our single breath. We heaved slowly and in unison. Invisible catapults, onagers, or some other medieval siege equipment of our imaginings hurled the chunks. Into the air each piece sprang, seeming to us then as big as a boulder, brilliant with nooks of tar.

When they hit the snake, they sent it frenzied into the shallow water, the water still building with each second. And because we were boys, we each yelled, *Fuck,* slowly, but then ran quickly without looking back. We weren't laughing this time at all. At one point we slowed from cramps, a stitch in each side, and Hill, the slowest of us at that point, yelled, It's chasing us! Like a pack of hound dogs suddenly picking up a scent, we were off again, bounding through the water, praying aloud that no other danger lay in wait.

When we finally reached the dock, we were breathless. We stopped and then, again in unison, dropped our free hand onto a knee and sucked in the suffocating smell of rot and stagnation the exposed banks now mixed with the building tide. Glen was the first to laugh, which put us at ease. We joined him. I think it was the first time in my life I actually guffawed.

Did you see him running? I said, catching my breath. I pointed back at Hill.

Me? Hill said, just now reaching us. I didn't see any of you pussies walking back there.

Shit, Glen said.

It went back and forth this way. Our cajoling, pushing one another, popping each other in the head, and things like that, no one noticing a nearly submerged coffee can had tipped over near Glen's foot. Um, he said. *Fellas?*

You could tell from the way his voice cracked that it wasn't puberty at work. It was simply the ease at which terror can enter us at any age. After that, Glen didn't speak. We immediately saw what had startled him.

In an almost perfect circle, there were five baby water moccasins. Except for their spaded heads and longer undulant tails, they actually looked like tadpoles. They treaded in place, as if in formation. The water had settled from how still each of us was at that moment.

The baby snakes were too small to affect a current, but we knew, in what we'd memorized from field guides and other manuals of the outdoors, how the young were born poisonous. It didn't seem fair to me that anyone or anything could be fated with venom, to have to wield it whether you wanted to or not. Still, we thought it was pretty cool.

Glen had by now become a statue. His outstretched arm ran parallel to the glassy surface. The water reflected clouds on which the baby moccasins flew. At one point, they were no longer snakes. They became exclamation points rippling on end.

Perhaps we understood what was at stake if we chose not to act fast. We each spoke slowly the directions. Our voices blurring until it was just one voice:

Glen, on the count of three, you run, okay? *One.*

What are you guys doing? he said, his eyes widening.

Two. We lifted each bucket over our head.

Shit, he said and sprang forward.

Three!

Before the word had left our mouths, Glen was already on the dock, more a crane in repose than a boy of thirteen. We were there as well. The minnows we had taken time to gather were the only things absent.

Slider

John, my closest friend growing up, will tell you my father taught him how to throw a slider, or maybe it was a breaking ball. I don't remember which one. You will have to ask John. I do remember times in our backyard, my uniform jersey and white pants with the bunched ends above the ankles hanging on the line. Gusts would send the tethered clothing parallel to the bent heads of grass. It almost seemed to be from his pitching, for John could bring the heat, his fastball always stinging my catcher's mitt.

He would be in the near distance, starting his wind-up to zing one at me, my father standing beside him talking quietly and exercising patience. It helped, too, that I had made All Stars as a catcher, because I would snag even the wild ones destined for our house behind me. An odd fact about our shared childhood is that throughout our years playing organized ball, John and I would never play on the same team. Each time at bat, I would stand at the plate, ready to face whatever he pulled out of his bag of numerous tricks. He would be on the mound laughing at me and shaking his head, his hand behind his back rolling the ball into place.

Though I had seen his pitches a thousand times or more, I could stand there and feel my breathing quicken. I was nervous. I knew he was as well. I tracked the curve's swing, but then, as if my legs didn't work, found myself waiting, wincing before the ball rocketed against my back or my side, and I inevitably yelled fuck in every room of my head.

Only once did I ever get a hit off John. It was one of the last games I would ever play. A night game with bats in the distance swooping below the outfield's tall mast of overhead lights. John had already hit me earlier in the game. My second at bat was different. He was on the mound snickering again, embarrassed, I knew, and I was shaking my head, smiling, like we were sharing the punch line of an inside joke. Aside from his propensity for wild pitches (but just with me), John had a fast release. If you didn't concentrate, you would only be swinging at air.

I watched his familiar wind-up. His stout body leaned over and locked into position like a cannon. The ball stalled over the plate for a split second. It wasn't until I watched the second baseman jump and miss that I realized I had actually gotten a good piece of it. I rounded first and stood up at second. John turned around and looked at me. We were both smirking at one another, then we laughed.

First Time

The first time I put one out of the park, she was there with some of her friends, older girls who would see me at the house and would wink at me and tell Rica how cute I was. I had put the ball over the left field fence at B. M. Williams ballpark. Had sent it with a clean stroke.

It surprised me more than anything. When I saw the ball sail over the last lifted glove, I looked at Rica and she was grinning and holding onto her friends' hands and jumping up and down. I imagined myself Mike Schmidt of the real Phillies smacking one into the upper deck.

That year Rica would try out for the cheerleading squad at Great Bridge High School, but already she had the natural ability to build excitement for those strangers standing nearby. She was muscular and tan, and between the two of us, she looked more mixed. I know some people looked at her as though she were exotic. At that time we didn't know of any Filipinos in Great Bridge. All of our father's navy friends were either in Norfolk or Virginia Beach. My ninang and her family, who we usually visited for parties and gatherings, also lived in Virginia Beach.

I would see strangers, both men and women, do double takes when my sister passed them by. As her younger brother, I was used to it, though a part of me didn't like it. I understood, nonetheless. As I jogged around the bases in that moment, pausing when I rounded third and saw her face again, I could barely contain my joy and neither could she. I didn't care that the opposing team glared at me from their dugout in their meringue yellow A's jerseys.

I skipped the remaining stretch, kicking up the chalk line with my cleats. My teammates bounced up and down, straight and vertical, looking like photographs of the Masai in Africa I'd seen in copies of the *National Geographic* our mother kept religiously around the house. As if it weren't enough that our father was from another country, we had to be reminded the world was larger and more colorful than our little town.

It was also a rite of passage, this *out-of-the-park* homer. What made it so great was the wave of celebration that came with it. My teammates slapped hard the top of my batting helmet, the steady thunk of each hit ringing in my ears. Then there was the calm settling as I took my helmet off. I found her standing near the entrance of our dugout. Her arms were open, and the bright world blurred behind her.

The Clothespin

It was the year the house always smelled like cabbage. She had read about it, or she knew a girl from school who had tried it and now swore by it. There was always a pair of jeans that she needed to fit into. That, or a bikini. The cabbage would be the answer, the salvation.

It involved filling the deep black pot we normally used to steam crabs, bushels our mother would bring back from roadside stands in North Carolina, that we'd redden with Old Bay and boiling water. The cabbage came from roadside stands too, I think. Rippled heads dropped into the dark gurgling water, softening. They released the ill fragrance of my sister's desire to be thin. It's sad to think about now, but I know it consumed her.

Tinah, my oldest sister, was less affected by this craving to fit in. I don't want to say it was easier for her, because I'm sure it wasn't. At least not on the surface. With light brown hair and blue eyes, she was a product of our mother's first marriage and looked more like our first cousins at family gatherings than Rica and I ever would. It is no surprise to anyone in our family that Tinah was our father's favorite. She was *Ate*, the oldest daughter, and our father insisted we treat her with the respect Filipino families afforded the eldest.

Perhaps a portion of Rica's obsession to be thin and glamorous had to do with her being mestiza, part-Filipino. Already an obvious outsider in a community where at that time you were either white or black or some close version of the two. If you were mixed, though, people loved to ask you where you were from. When you said, *Here*, they would shake their head as if saying, Don't be silly, you know what I mean. And when you'd finally answer, *My father is from the Philippines*, they would smile knowingly and nod, as if saying, See, that wasn't so hard now, was it?

Issues of *Cosmo* lay dog-eared and wrinkled on Rica's bed. They were opened to articles on how to look sexy, or things to do to drive a guy wild. Pictures of models were circled with markers. I remember Christie Brinkley had endless black spirals around her. Before this magazine, she read *Seventeen* and taped *Tiger Beat* pullout posters of Leif Garrett or John Travolta to the back of her bedroom door. I remember Tinah was going to marry Parker Stevenson, and Rica was going to marry Shaun Cassidy. Or maybe it was the other way around.

At nights I would walk into the bathroom and find Rica staring at herself in the mirror. She might be plucking at an obstinate eyebrow or filing her nails, which she kept long and polished and immaculate. Inevitably, she would complain to her reflection, usually about her hair, which she thought was more like horsehair, coarse and thick and black and unruly. In many ways, she was the quintessential teenage American girl—a lingering aversion for most versions of the way she looked. Rarely was she satisfied with her figure, though I always saw her as athletic and lithe.

Most brothers have lots of dirt on their older sisters. That is, if they have older sisters. It is one of the natural laws of this world. I remember coming home one evening after a long game of neighborhood football, my face still tingling from the cool night air, from running headlong into a shadow of bodies that dispersed into boys and voices. My sense of smell was especially acute.

I could smell the sweet, itchy cool scent of freshly mown grass, the shredded stalks of milkweed that marked the unkempt regions of property lines. When I walked into our house, I felt faint from the noxious fumes coming from the kitchen.

The house smelled like piss. Like boiled vinegar and piss. You could stand at the front door and feel the laced steam against your face. I cupped my mouth and forced my way into the kitchen where I found Rica stirring near the steamy cauldron.

She looked more like a witch at that moment than my sister. I almost yelled out, but coughed instead. When she turned around to face me, I saw her black mess of hair was held back with a headband. I froze. On her nose was a clothespin. At first I thought she had worn the clothespin because the fumes were too much. This thought struck me, but I laughed anyway. Only afterwards, when she had settled down with a bowl of this broth, did I notice she didn't take off the clothespin. It stayed on. It wasn't for the cabbage at all. It was for her nose. She thought the pinching would straighten it, make it less flat. She thought, if she tried, she could become someone else entirely.

Punker

I had come back from playing at Hill's house. We had tried to perfect spirals, launching ovals that spun through paths of slick air. They carried, and we would run under each one, speeding then slowing, compensating so as not to get ahead of these passes as they began their descent through the canopy of pines and into our nimble fingers.

Back at the house, I found Rica taking a marker to her jeans. She was writing a band's name on one of the knees. The B-52's in bright red. Then she took a pair of scissors and clipped a small incision in which she fished in her fingers and began to pull, ripping a long tear in the side. On the bed beside her was a T-shirt; she had shredded the sleeves. The rest of it was now laid out looking as though she might put an iron on it and smooth what little fabric was left unmarred.

What are you doing? I said. I glanced around the room to see if any other damage had been done. Her posters were hanging in their same spots, the faux-antique telephone still in place. Onyx, her Persian cat, lay curled in the corner of the room and blinked at me slowly, as if bored with my presence. It all but yawned.

Rica, I said.

What? she said, ripping another slit in her jeans. She was concentrating, being strategic, I could tell. She went over the words in marker again and bore down harder. If I squinted, the words looked more like a swathe spattering of blood.

What are you doing? I said.

What do you mean? she said, smiling. I'm fixing my clothes. What does it look like I'm doing?

I shook my head. Fixing for what? I said.

For school, she said.

C'mon.

I'm serious, she said. Tomorrow's the start of Spirit Week. I'm going as a punker.

What's a *punker*? I said. It would be a few more years before I'd discover Sid Vicious and Johnny Rotten and those wonderful Sex Pistols' anthems.

What's a punker, she said and pushed me.

I'm serious, I said, unaware that The Clash record I cranked at night was in any way tied to the scene. She didn't tell me.

It's an angry kid, I guess, she said. Just an angry kid.

Altar Boys

Someone thought it would be a good idea to let the altar boys have a day at the beach. They gathered us together and took us to Little Island, at the far end of Sandbridge. It was Saturday, warm, but I remember not really wanting to go, because I knew some of the older boys had a penchant for cruelty.

When we would gather before Mass and put on thin white robes over our clothes, the older ones wouldn't think twice about giving you titty twisters or smacking your head and trying to provoke you. The entire time they would be laughing and saying, Just kidding, as if that excused any action that preceded or ensued. It wasn't all of them, just a few, but of course all it took was one and inevitably others would join in. What made it worse was that I wasn't in school with any of them. If there was a club among the altar boys, I was without doubt the outsider.

The day we went to the beach, it was after a storm and there were jellyfish that had washed onto the shore. If you went into the surf, which was considerably colder than the air, you risked getting stung. Most of us went anyway. We dove into the faces of waves rippled with those glasslike bodies. When we surfaced, we found ourselves farther out. I considered myself a strong swimmer. The current, though, could never be trusted. I wasn't as adventurous as the others, many of whom disappeared into the shore break and became hard to track, especially if you were trying to keep your eye right on them.

At one point I joined some of the boys closer to my age, and we started digging quickly a hole that widened and deepened with each near reach of the approaching water. C'mon, c'mon, we all yelled at one another. Sand flew, and the waves kept threatening to wash away our good work. Mole crabs scurried from the damp clumps we freed, the sand dissolving back into the sand. Out of the corner of my eye, I could barely see the older boys. I knew they were laughing, could hear them practicing the maniacal laughter of late-night television monster movies. When they blurred I looked to find them beaming each other with globes of jellyfish, the bodies resembling in that instant translucent baseballs.

I knew when they had finished with one another they would go in search of some other excitement, something else to pelt or to destroy or both. The tallest kid, David, had grabbed one of the jellyfish, a large medusa, and was holding it upside down so that its reddish brown tentacles, some stringy as spaghetti, swayed away from his wrist. He held it with an air of ritual, like it was one of the trays we would use in a Sunday service to catch the wafers of Eucharist that might fall from someone's lips. Two of David's henchmen, their tangle of bangs covering their eyes, followed alongside him and bounced nervously, smiling, each mop of hair revealing a pair of black, beady eyes.

Who? Who? they asked David. They were dying to know.

Shut up, David said.

Tell us, tell us, they said.

Shut up, David said again and took his free hand and brought a finger to his lips. Shut the fuck up, all right?

At first I thought this last piece of anger was directed at me, because the two beside him lunged and grabbed at my legs, pulling me back. It was for the world in general. The henchmen held me while David pulled down the front of my shorts and placed the mass of tentacles there between my legs. He pressed hard the body against me and twisted the globe back and forth, like he was juicing halves of oranges gone clear and rancid.

From where I was sitting, the ocean shifted in slow motion. There was no sound, though I knew my mouth was open, and the feeling of paper ripping over and over was the way the air in my throat moved between what I thought must have been my screaming and what I was sure was my ruined breathing. Every boy was laughing, especially the smaller ones, who must have been relieved that I had been the only one chosen.

When David and the others were finished, they stood up and brushed the sand from their legs and stuck out their chests and swaggered as they punched each other in the arm, happy, satiated for the time being. I wasn't as calm. The air ripped open then, and the sound of things came rushing back. There was the distinct scrape of my fingers mindlessly pulling out chunks from inside my shorts. The jellyfish managed to sting me everywhere its tentacles could still slip in its microscopic barbs. It didn't matter that the thing itself was dead. My balls burned, and it was all I could do not to cry out. So I gingerly removed the smallish pieces left, whimpering as I did, and decided it would be best to simply brave the water, let it wash away the fragments from my skin.

So I did. While the others had made their way back to the group's spot of towels and things on the beach, I stood in the water and told myself I'd never do something like that to anyone. I meant the ridicule, but I didn't know the meaning of that word just yet.

Spirit

During the end of her freshman year, Rica bombed during cheering tryouts. Not to be defeated, though, she undertook, as most girls in this town had done before her (and happily afterward), the daunting task of long practices fueled only with hope. One year of continually falling and getting back up and going to bed hoarse from yelling cheers into the cool evenings of their neighborhoods. That is exactly what Rica did. There, into the darkening yard with our light blue water tower in the near distance, its single red light suddenly coming on like a signal of something approaching from above. Evening after evening, she would fade into the sky.

Days were spent in our backyard with the clothes pinned to the line and blowing in the wind, looking like the ghosts of spectators rippling in response. Rica would do cartwheels, one after the other. She would practice her cheers between chores. The words were sharp, clipped at the ends in her forceful renderings—Ready? O-kay. There were jumps called Russians, she quickly informed me.

And what's that one called? I said.

Herkie! She would tilt her hip in mid-air and her legs would slip into place under her. Landing, she'd do it again as if the grass were the stretched surface of a trampoline.

And what's that one called? I said, actually curious about the next jump.

A stag, she said. I didn't tell her they looked identical.

Whenever her friends came over, I was the entitled younger brother floating in and out to provide comic relief. If Rica was starting a cheer, I would mouth the words behind her. This usually brought a laugh. I couldn't resist. They were all teenage girls years older than me, and they were all beauties, every one of them. All to say it made my necessary and expected disruptions worthwhile.

Some of these girls were already varsity cheerleaders. They were as close to local royalty as one could get when it came to high school social hierarchy. Sad to say I knew this, even though I was in middle school at the time. Rica was so determined to make the squad, she had filled me in. Anything that could capture her imagination to this extreme had to be something more than simply wanting to fit in. Still, there was no denying their long legs and tight bodies. Their wavy, feathered hair. What girl didn't want to be the object of so much attention? At least it's what I thought. Sometimes the girls would come to the house and stay for hours, and I would catch glimpses of them primping after having just run through a routine, as if part of their workout involved also retaining a sense of glamour.

In summer months it was more difficult. Our town, located on the southeastern tip of Virginia, is infamous for its humid weather. These girls would try to stay cool in the shade while one would inevitably lead them in one of the latest cheers or demonstrate one of the more difficult jumps. The louder you were, the more spirit you had. That was one of the things I quickly learned from my sister was revered — Spirit.

After these girls left, my sister would stay outside and practice. It would be thundering, and she wouldn't budge. It would start sprinkling, and still she was dead set on continuing. And though she floated at times above the grass, harnessing a rare moment of grace, other times she fell, and fell hard. She would get up, though, and brush herself off. Countless times she would wipe her face before assuming a smile. I never knew at whom she was smiling. Then the routine again. It was always the routine one had to perfect.

That spring of her sophomore year, Rica's hard work paid off. Our mother had gone up to the high school for the tryouts. She was sitting in the bleachers of the gymnasium with the other parents and the cliques of students who had chosen their favorites and were screaming their names before the girls even performed their first cheers. Our mother recalls being nervous, gripping her fingers as she watched each girl perform a series of stunts. One of them almost tripped. It was Rica. They continued on, and once the girls were finished, the crowd gave them all a standing ovation. *We were both crying,* our mother says when she thinks about that day. *She stuck with it and made it.*

A year later Rica would finish the cheering season and move right into playing wing on the varsity girls' soccer team. She would manage this, even though she had never played organized soccer before. It didn't matter to her that she wasn't exceptional at the sport, only that she got a chance to compete and spend time with friends, Ellen being one of them. That same semester she would be competing in the Miss Great Bridge pageant, garnering a nod for Miss Congeniality. Her excitement for simply having been part of it all seemed, even then to me, to be something worth remembering. She was a determined person, and this trait, little did we know then, would serve her to the end.

II.

An Endless Retelling

Friends and family had packed into our home to celebrate. Our mother had spent the night before getting things ready. Lots of cooking, lots of rearranging one covered casserole dish after the next onto the bowing shelves of our green refrigerator. In each dish were lined rows of lumpia, Filipino eggrolls, and in the deeper ones pancit and chicken adobo. There was also a pot of collard greens seasoned with salted ham and a huge bowl of mustard-based potato salad covered with a crinkled sheet of aluminum foil. In the oven rested a pan of homemade buttermilk biscuits. Some of these dishes had to be reheated, but it didn't matter. There was so much food. Too much.

Even so, our mother kept cooking, busying herself as she prepared fresh meals and set plates of steamy noodles mixed with soy sauce and cooked garlic slices, bowls of fried rice on the nicked wooden table that had to be widened with a leaf in the center. Raised on a farm in North Carolina, our mother knew how to cook Southern, but she had also learned to prepare Filipino dishes from the wives she had met and befriended living on naval bases along the East Coast. With no air conditioning in the house, fans ticked in corners, clicking at intervals to push the warm air around from one person to the next. When the heat gathered around us, we waved it away like it was an incessant fly. Everywhere was the smell of garlic, in the air and in each conversation.

While our mother moved about the kitchen, laughing at whatever anyone said, our father sat in the living room with his hands on his knees. At this point our parents had been separated for nearly two years, but for reasons still unknown to me, they had not yet divorced. I remember my father kept his suit coat on for his entire stay that night, or at least, whenever I would walk in to see how he was doing, I found him bundled and sitting on the edge of one of the recliners. He looked ready to run off at any moment.

Boo, he said. Go get your sister.

Which one? I said. I hadn't seen Tinah yet and suspected she was off with her boyfriend, Eddie, delaying her arrival. This was her graduation party, after all. She would show at some point. I could hear our mother's voice above the others in the kitchen. Though he was smiling, my father looked annoyed.

Go get Rica, my father said and gestured to the other room with arched eyebrows and a jolt of the neck. I had seen other Filipinos motion with their lips, but my father never seemed to fully embrace this style of gesturing. His seemed more a functional hybridization, a subtlety better suited to his more serious nature.

Ellen, Rica's friend, had graduated that night as well and was there in our kitchen. She was still wearing her white graduation gown, which had a silver sheen to it from the way the light played against the warbling fabric. Like my sister Rica, Ellen was a pretty girl with a big smile and feathered dark auburn hair. I didn't know if it was her natural color, but if she shared Rica's obsession for makeup and glamour, Ellen's hair color was probably due to an overzealous application of lemon juice and sunshine.

I found Rica smiling with her arm around Ellen. Anyone could see that these girls were friends. Our mother, with her apron still tied around the dress she had worn to the ceremony, was snapping a picture of the two of them. In lime green slacks and a yellow Izod shirt, my friend John, with his back to them, is leaning across the platters of food to reach the mound of lumpia. This photograph now rests behind a brittle sheet of plastic, in an album that moves surreptitiously throughout the various rooms of our mother's house. As if buoyant the book of photographs will resurface for one of us to thumb through at our family gatherings now. It is the last picture we have of Rica before the accident. I think it is also the last picture of Ellen as well.

I walked back into the living room, and my father just looked at me like I was supposed to hand him something. I know all night he hasn't made his way into the kitchen, which makes me wonder if I should ask if he's hungry. But I don't. I just stand there, as if blocking him from my mother's view, and him from hers. It is the role I have learned to play, to be the go-between in their continual drama.

What's your sister doing? he says.

Taking pictures, I say.

Tell her to come here, he says. You tell her I want to talk to her.

In our family history there are two stories about the ensuing conversation that night between Rica and my father. Both have survived in their endless retelling. In my father's version all he knows is that he doesn't want her to go to Nags Head. He has a bad feeling about all of it. He knows the other high school kids are renting cottages and going down to the beach for the week, and he knows they will be partying and that there will be alcohol. He doesn't want his youngest daughter in the middle of it.

This is your sister Tinah's year, he tells her. *Next year, you can go.*

He knows our mother has already agreed to let her go with her friend Ellen. Because our father no longer lives in this house, he finds his authority has been lessened by his absence. He knows after tonight Rica will get to go no matter what he says, but even knowing this, he makes one last attempt. He offers to give her five hundred dollars to go shopping with so long as she doesn't leave for North Carolina. Rica pauses, smiles. She loves shopping for clothes. He knows this.

In my mother's version, which claims Rica as the source, Rica goes in search of our father and finds him the same as I have, uneasy and out of place in the house he had helped build for this family. Rica hugs him and says, I want you to know that I *know* you love me. The insinuation, of course, is that he didn't show her, that she is the one showing him now. I don't know how much of this is our mother's revision and how much of it is what really happened. Either way, both versions end with our father speech-less, without a voice.

My Father, in Some Small Corner of Memory

I don't remember if I called him. Maybe he just happened to be calling the house at the time. I know he was in Bayonne, where he had been living and working in New Jersey. I remember, too, the local news stations were airing reports about four students from Great Bridge involved in a fatal car crash down in the Outer Banks. On TV one reporter decided to stand next to the cloth-covered wreckage. I saw large maroon blots on the canvas tarp. I wondered why they would feel it necessary to show my sister's blood to the world.

When I heard my father's voice, I immediately said, Dad, but then my heart sank.

Boo, what's going on? he said. His voice was nervous, shaky, like he already knew something bad had happened.

Rica was in a bad accident, I said. A car accident. I could barely speak. My voice felt thin, like a piece of crumpled paper that kept needing to be smoothed. Or a wafer dissolving on the tongue. I could feel it all disappearing, my voice especially, but not before I told him her head had been hurt, that it had *opened some*.

This last part made him cry.

I started crying too, because I had made my father cry. I was a boy who had made his father cry. I didn't know the exact details of Rica's injury. I was simply the bearer of the burden my father could now begin to carry himself. I knew a dump truck filled with sand had crushed the small Datsun my sister had ridden in. The dump truck had actually vaulted halfway over the car and halted, grinding the car down before eventually stopping altogether. Lots of her classmates were there to witness the accident.

We would learn later how, because of the impact and the coiling and fusing of these vehicles, it would take rescue workers nearly thirty-five minutes to jack up the truck so the medics could reach those trapped inside. I remember hearing my father cry and feeling as though I had done something wrong by telling him all that I knew. I should not have said the thing about her head opening.

My father, who is always so serious in my memories of him, is weeping into the phone hours away. I hold the receiver. I hold it to my ear and say, listening closely, *Dad, I know*, but I don't know. There is so much I will never know, and my father, in some small corner of memory, continues on with his weeping, and it is not for me, his oldest son, to stop him.

Translucent

There were students gathered in the waiting room and parents holding them as they sobbed. Everyone asked unanswerable questions and were shushed and soothed. Teenage girls wore T-shirts too big for their bodies, their bikini top straps peeked out above the stretched collars, and on their legs were patches of sand clinging to their tan or even burnt skin. Then various moments when clergy were leading groups in prayer. Something had been altered in these peoples' lives, and they wanted reassurance. Moments before, I had gone down the long, bright corridor and walked through the door to the ICU. There I met the image that would graft itself to my being.

Before I was pulled away, for I was too young to be in there, my eyes tracked the translucent blue snake that coiled in the air above my sister's throat. I would later learn it was for Rica's tracheotomy. As for her face, it was puffy and bruised, deformed. More like a boxer's face that had been beaten beyond the bell one too many times, like a face I had seen at one of the boxing matches my father had taken me to down at the Amphibious Base in Little Creek. But my sister's was worse.

Her hair had been shaved on one side, and what was left was lopsided and looked enraged. She didn't move. Though broken, her body held her in place. In that time before my sister's condition stabilized, days and nights gained and lost momentum depending

upon the medical team's next course of action. Hope, it seemed
to me even then, was doled out in small doses, like medication. In
the waiting rooms many lined up to learn the latest, only to find
out it was contingent upon the success of some procedure or some
unpredictable outcome. Either progress or regress, movement or
stasis, this news felt random, instead of fixed to something cosmic,
the way the tidal waters were to the moon.

When they finally moved her to her own room, where we could
see her and touch her, she remained in a deep sleep. A coma, one
of the doctors explained. It was the first time I had heard the word
coma. It seemed like such a strange word, too, just a letter away
from comma. Comma seemed more fitting, a visual pause in the
sentence of her life. The room blinked from the bouquet of red
and violet lights, the mechanisms at work to cycle air in and out of
my sister's ruptured lungs. Looking at this body I had to believe it
still held Rica somewhere in the realm of its dreaming.

I wanted her to wake, and I wanted to wake as well.

Diorama

You take a shoebox and line the inside with black construction paper, gluing the back of each small sheet and pressing it until you feel the clumps begin to seep. You make angled cuts into folded squares of aluminum foil. Almost like you're making snowflakes. There is uniformity in the stars you hang with the clear fishing line.

Behind the ruffled green paper segments taped to one another and then to the front edge of the shoebox, you place the magazine cutout of Christie Brinkley face down. The typed words on the page opposite the image will resemble the engraved headstones you've seen flush with the ground in various graveyards. You have stopped playing with G.I. Joes, but you take one out of the toy box in your brothers' room, which is the room you share with them, and place the soldier on top of these words, where the image of a woman rests underneath. When you're done, you go back into her room and you set the diorama to the side and get down on your knees and tell God that all you want is for her to live and not die. That's all you and everyone else wants. Then you make the sign of the cross out of habit.

You have already heard the way it happened, the way it might have happened, but here is how it happened, or at least how you now think it happened. No one will tell you she folded herself around the boy in the backseat. She didn't mean to, but the truck had hit them with such force that the impact threw her body into the air, and so she thought it best to give in to the momentum, if she thought anything at all. The two of them spun and wrapped farther around one another, like a pair of twins in utero, and before the rescue workers could pry the dump truck from the car, those standing nearby could already see the dark red wet on the road. In each place it landed on the pavement, it spread its tiny fingers wide as if to reach.

When they finally pulled her from the car, she was wearing nothing except a T-shirt of blood. And they had to pry her hands away from her broken face. An impulse for vanity or otherwise, it didn't matter now. It saved her to some degree. On her face they found the dumb expression of one not only knocked unconscious, her mouth open and her eyes dipped back, but also of one ecstatic, like Saint Theresa, her body looking ravaged completely by the Spirit.

Those nearby would not look at her legs and think of her legs around them, around their waists, pulling them to her and pushing away and then pulling, back and forth, the blood this thing between them. They would not see the others and think of them as friends they had partied with the night before, the celebrations still fizzing around in the core of each stunned brain. Instead, they would later repeat the rumor that one had ridden a few cars back and just before the accident traded into the car that would not see the dump truck until it was too late.

Or not that way at all, but this way: Where there is always distance to cross. In her room, back in Chesapeake, is a green and gold megaphone with the bubbly letters of her cursive on a small sheet of paper taped near the worn metal handle. On the paper are the words in blue ink to cheers she should know, but she keeps them there to remind herself. She has said these words and released them into Friday nights, under the lights of football stadiums, the words becoming clouds. That same mouth, that smile. Within it the voice that would bore into the vortex of our longing. That voice would be loudest in silence, just before the endless chorus of *Oh Shit!* or *Fuck it!* or *Fuck me!* or *Oh, my God!* or *Please God!* or just *God!* and then the crushing growl of the truck's grill as it pokes its muzzle into where they are.

Or not that way either, but this way, yes, this way: Someone on the beach sees in the distance helicopters descend beyond the bending fence of sea oats, where the beach is no longer real, was never real. And the helicopters then vanish, become the period at the end of this sentence.

An Entire Life Story, Instead of a Loaf of Bread

For months, Rica slept. The room where she lay had a wall of glass that looked out onto the nurses' station. On the other walls of her room our mother had taped cards and pictures sent in from relatives and friends, even from people we didn't know but who prayed for my sister. I know to think of people doing so comforted our mother beyond words. Balloons and arrangements, various stuffed animals stayed with her as she slept, as did our mother, as much as she could be away from her other children. Tinah, I know, was also there.

I remember one of the doctors had told our mother we should talk to Rica, that even in a coma she could hear us. We didn't know if it would really do any good, but we hoped it would. If anything, we were still filled with hope. Our mother was convinced it would do our sister good, so we did. We talked to her. We told her everything. We mentioned what the weather was like, even if it was uneventful. We talked about movies that were in the theaters, songs that were on the radio. The most mundane subjects one might normally overlook did not go unspoken of. We thumbed through magazines and commented sarcastically on the various advertisements. We included her as we scoffed at the programs on TV, at the inane news, at whatever the world felt was important at the time.

But for us, nothing was more important than having her wake.

That was it. The most Rica would do in response was to flutter her eyes at the sound of our voices. This is what we thought. We weren't sure if it was out of boredom or if it was her only way to plead we should quit. In my mind, if she was in a coma, it meant she was sleeping, and if she was sleeping, then at some point, she had to be dreaming. I would sit in the chair beside her and just stare at the cards on the wall. Time in the hospital became blocks of nothingness. Intervals between IV bag changes and a flourish of beeps. Elevator rides down to the cafeteria and rides back up to the room, and the nurses trying to be pleasant when I filed by the station and saw her blurry form and prayed a small prayer back when I believed that prayers were answered.

At first I couldn't bring myself to talk to her. I felt silly, like she would wake at any moment and say in a disappointed tone, *Boo, what are you doing?* When I did talk to her, it was usually because our mother was in the room, and I knew she expected it of us. But talking came easy to our mother. Having been raised in a small farming town in North Carolina, she carried with her through life an inherent belief that when she met someone, and it could be anyone, she should know something about them. Not in a nosy way, but in a familiar way, like she would remember it for the next time their paths crossed.

Our mother's job before Rica's accident had been as a checkout cashier at Farm Fresh, one of the grocery stores in the area. In many ways it was a perfect arrangement. It gave our mother a chance to meet all kinds of people and to do so in both a public as well as an intimate setting, with the food they ate and all of the personal items they needed gliding on the wide conveyor belt between them.

Many nights our mother would come home and tell us stories about the people she had met, and when she mentioned something they might have said, she would relay the stories as if they had been passed on to her by old friends. Complete strangers would confess things to her, and she soaked in the attention. At the same time, she could walk into a store with the sole intent of purchasing something specific, something as simple as a loaf of bread. Then, as was sometimes the case, she would leave having completely forgotten her reason for going into the store in the first place, and yet she would have stopped to talk to at least one of the workers there and would know their names. She would know where they grew up, whether or not any of their ancestors were Irish or Cherokee, how many grandchildren they had, basically their entire life stories. Where I lacked in the ability to think of things to say, our mother made up for it by hovering nearby Rica and every now and then interjecting with cues.

Tell your sister what you want for your birthday, she'd say.

I would just look at our mother.

Well, she'd say, tell her about one of your baseball games.

Baseball was the one sport I had loved dearly, had started playing in a pitching league at five years old. Just a few months before, I had been chosen to represent my school, Crestwood Elementary, in the All-City Band Ensemble. It was a prestigious honor to have been selected, but instead of going to the final concert, the one that really mattered, I went to Opening Day at the baseball field.

There was something magical about wearing your new uniform and seeing the other teams gathered and running around, the ball caps bright and glowing in the sunlight. And I can still see Mr. K—, my sixth-grade band teacher, his usually pasty pale skin reddening as he yelled at me after class that following Monday. He kept asking what was wrong with me.

Don't you realize the horrible thing you've done? he said, over and again. Don't you? *Don't you?*

He wasn't content, I think, until he made me cry—which he did. Only I was really crying for another reason entirely. My father no longer lived with us, and one of the things he and I had shared early on, the closest thing to sacred I could name at that age, could be found on that field, on Opening Day.

The First Dream

I dreamt I woke and found my father puttering around our kitchen, like he was known to do before he left us. It would be autumn, and he would be wearing a sweatshirt tucked into his sweatpants, and over his sweatpants he would wear a pair of pastel blue shorts with fuzzy white piping trim. He looked like a Filipino version of Rocky Balboa before the character's famous run through the streets of . Philadelphia, where he ended up on those wide steps overlooking the city and fake punching and shuffling and throwing his arms in the air to celebrate some victory.

But this was Chesapeake, Virginia, outside the town of Great Bridge. If there were a shuffling sound to be heard, it would be only that of my father's black faux leather slip-on sandals scooting across the new linoleum, from our lima bean green refrigerator to the stove top and back to the open door of the refrigerator again.

He would be intent on cooking breakfast. Steamed white rice in a pot with a sweet glaze bubbling off and warming the room, and in the pan beside it, slices of bologna frying in pink half moons. The moons popping in the grease would curl at the edges and were more like wings really, like the wings of skates you might see at Virginia Beach in late summer, the skates thrashing about in some drawn out ritual on the ocean's surface.

Though I didn't speak the language, I would say to my father, Magandang umaga. I would know it meant *good morning*. He would look up then like he had just heard one of his navy buddies calling to him. Maybe even another Filipino from the same province, from Nueva Ecija. But the moment he saw my face, he would shrug like he didn't know Tagalog or, worse, like he didn't know me, his firstborn son.

And though, in my dream, I could finally be fluent in my father's language, it would not be his language anymore. I would know this. I would not be his son. It was as if I understood that my changing had changed him and likewise. Any transformation involved great risks. My sister Rica left the house one day and didn't return for months, and when she finally did, she was someone else entirely.

I've had this dream more than once, though as I've grown older, I'm sure I willed the subsequent ones. There is sustenance in each, I suppose. In another version Rica is at the table. She is sitting in her wheelchair, but even though I can't exactly make out her full form, I know it is her before the car accident. She's the one that greets me when I walk into the kitchen, sounding like an exchange on language tapes I've listened to more than once:

Magandang umaga — *Good morning*.

Magandang umaga. Kumusta ka? — *Good morning. How are you?*

Mabuti — *I'm fine*.

Our father, without looking up, goes about his task of preparing her the same meal. Steamed rice that he'll put in a bowl and add milk. The milk will warm and sweeten from the steamed rice. The bologna will be burnt along the edges, like the wings have fallen from a great height and burned during their descent.

Before our father can finish fixing her plate, she stands up and walks
out. Palaam na, she says and waves. She leaves us both alone with
the wheelchair I know is not really there. My father is singing a
song that is neither sad nor happy. But he is singing, and I recognize
it as such. It is a lament that is not fully a lament, a lament yet to
become a lament. I know that I don't need to know the words.

A Collective Forgetting

He would have passed dinosaurs and other animals, the painted fiberglass ones, muscular but harmless. All were attractions for one of the local family restaurants. The dinosaurs would have still been there in some form, as would the wooden signs of vegetables drawn with painted smiles and big lashy eyes staked in succession as he drove south, the only route leading to the bridge across the Albemarle Sound. This route was lined with roadside vegetable stands: mounds of snap beans, sweet Silver Queen corn, sweet potatoes, and squash, all types from the squat bulbs to the coiled, overgrown cashew-shaped Butternut variety.

He might have felt each stand ticking quietly in the periphery of his vision, the two-way road that was the bridge then doling out in small yellow lines no bigger than bricks, tempting anyone to count them down to their destination. He might have wondered then, crossing the bridge, at the oncoming traffic threatening with each pass his own small Datsun hatchback, the little brown car that would last him another twenty years.

He would reach the intersection in Southern Shores, North Carolina, but he could just as easily be in St. Peter's basilica again, staring at the light slipping on the marble skin of Michelangelo's famous Pietá. He would gaze up at the stop sign, in a confused awe that it could exist, that it had come from nothing and had affected everything. It was the stop sign that did not stop the car that held his daughter, the car that later cradled her like a hand closing, cupping her and the shattering glass that spread across her like a blanket, as if she might sleep within it.

I'm not sure how long he stayed there. He's told me since that he went just to see the place, see for himself the intersection where the driver, a girl who only weeks before the accident received her license, had brought the car into the path of an oncoming dump truck. He wanted to see the highway with traffic speeding by, cars filled with families going north or south. If you drove south, you would find the road eventually ends after Buxton. You would come to the small ferry station and onto a ramp that leads to the flat boat itself—perhaps you will ride the *Chicamacomico* all the way to Ocracoke Island.

If you go north, though, you go back to the bridge that allows you to cross the Albemarle Sound again. The road returns you to the drive past farmlands and nearly neon green fields of soybean and corn, the long road heading back past Currituck and even Great Bridge. Eventually, you must leave your daughter in a hospital in Norfolk, where she sleeps without meaning to sleep. The coma becomes a collective forgetting for all, a pause in what to remember. You will leave the region where you lived most of your life as a father, to your new work in New Jersey. North where the road branches into other roads before you and becomes more lanes, numerous and entangled, and finally at the end to where you've driven, there is the apartment, where once you reach it, you slide the key into the lock, turn it, push open the door. You are greeted by the warm scent of your things. They've been sitting here in the dark, in the light. They've been waiting for you to come home and give them meaning.

Yellow

It's 2 a.m., and I'm with John and his father on a pier snaking out
into Lynnhaven Bay. The lights in the distance are of those that
mark the sections of the Chesapeake Bay Bridge. If you follow them
with your eyes, they yellow and then disappear into long patches
of nothing. That's where the tunnels take over, where travelers slip
their cars through the tubes heading away from Virginia Beach
for the Eastern Shore.

John and I leave his father to watch over the poles, their tips
bending at intervals from the current. When we'd first started
coming out here years ago, I would mistake the bending for a hit
and would shamelessly begin reeling in my line only to find the
hooks of my rig empty, the rig itself spinning like a mobile above a
crib. John wanted to see what others were pulling in, so we started
our walk, shuffling from person to person, quietly peering into
open coolers and tall buckets. Those fishing were mostly men,
older than John's father, and had weathered faces that rivaled the
gray chipped planks lining the pier.

They shared the characteristics of old sea captains who long
since lost command of ancient ships. We had learned there was
an etiquette to exchanges. If you were a kid, you didn't just start
speaking to anyone. It was usually their initiating what would
ultimately be a terse conversation. *Mornin'*, they said, and we'd
nod, smile with hands thrust in our wind breakers, the stiff salt

air tightening our faces. We'd put our backs to it as we spoke.

Any luck? we'd offer, the wind lifting our hoods and slapping them against our necks. The men would usually say a few names, mostly bait fish, and others that weren't good to eat. But if we'd hear the word *flounder*, we'd want to look at the fish's flat speckled body, its eyes crowded on one side above its odd, crooked mouth. The flounder was the only fish we'd keep. The others we caught we'd give away.

Once, near the end of the pier, we found a skate someone had pulled up. They'd cut off its barbed tail. The rest of its fanned body appeared fused to the boards, flush despite the buckled sections. I remember crouching beside the skate and counting the numerous slits made by a small knife. Those slits resembled dashes — *one — after — another*. So much so that if there were a meaningful pattern to the violence, I couldn't detect it. Years later, on a high school field trip to an anatomy lab, I would lean close to a woman splayed on a table and make out the initials someone had carved into her sunken cheek. Someone had taken a pen and had even drawn a smiley face next to the grim engraving. I learned from the lab attendant that this woman had died in a car accident. No one had claimed the body. *This*, the attendant said, *was not uncommon.*

In the corner another body sat wrapped in plastic. Though the plastic was translucent, looking more like a grimy shower curtain, you could see the chest and the torso and head. It was a man's face staring at you through the plastic. After a moment, you realize the body has been cut in half. The man is holding each of his severed legs like they're a pair of skis, like he is about to take on the triple black diamond downhill. Your imagination.

Human Chain

A few months after Rica's accident, my mother wanted to do something that felt normal. I could sense it in the way she spoke about my approaching birthday, about plans she wanted to make regardless of the fact that my sister was still in a coma. It was late August, and in what I imagine was a forced break away, my mother took me and two friends, John and Tommy, down to Nags Head. She wanted us to enjoy a day at the beach, maybe have a seafood dinner at one of the restaurants along the main road.

I remember seeing the intersection as we turned onto the main road. The car had since been removed. On the TV news reports, most of the local stations had felt inclined to broadcast the image of the cloth-covered wreckage, though there could have been anything under there. Holes poked in the soiled cloth were not unlike those on the hooded figure of David Lynch's *The Elephant Man*. No matter the comparison, I was equally held by the car's absence as we passed. I didn't look at my mother. I couldn't. There was only the laughter of my best friend, John, nudging me to trade off ridiculous *Your Mama* jokes (*Shut up, your mama's so fat, she got chin hairs the size of shoestrings*). In this realm, I was partially grounded. The rest of me wandered among those ruins of what my family would never fully recover, never fully understand.

The day itself was humid. The air a stagnant veil that stretched from Great Bridge to the Outer Banks, even though at the beach

the waves were choppy, signaling at least on the surface the shifting winds. My mother had set down a blanket on one part of the
beach, and John, Tommy, and I wandered off in search of girls our
age or, even better, older ones. In all of our horseplay and banter,
I'm not sure if we actually disregarded the red warning flags, or if
it was merely oversight that John and I sauntered into the water,
leaving Tommy behind. I know my mother must have seen the
water's tumult and been lulled by it. It was the landscape that
never stayed the same.

I'll admit that it was part of the attraction for me, the ocean's
hypnotism at work. Farther down the beach, John and I laughed
as we were swept within the onshore break. The current gripped
our waists and hoisted us through the faces of oncoming waves.
A few years before, John and I had taken swim lessons at the local
Y, had even surpassed the others in our class, those struggling as
Guppies and Minnows while John and I had tested into Sharks.
We never looked back at our classmates still doggie paddling. We
could zip underwater like a pair of torpedoes. It was a false sense
of confidence that must have propelled us into the surf that day,
with no regard whatsoever for rip currents or undertow. With each
undulant pass of waves, John and I started drifting farther apart.
Shut up, your mama's so fat, you use her toenail for a skimboard, one
of us would say, while the other one added, *Shut up, that's why your
grandma has eighteen toenails on one toe.*

Rarely did any of the jokes make sense.

I remember watching him become smaller, behind each growing wall of water. I yelled for him to swim back, to come closer to
where I was, but he only continued to diminish slowly. I could barely
hear him now. It was almost a disappearing act, one to be in awe
of were it not terrifying to witness its unfolding in slow motion. I
tried to swim out to him, but then a lifeguard coasted past me and
grabbed John, pulling him back into a shallow area. It wasn't until
I saw John stand that I realized he was growing smaller again.

I was the one now being pulled out by the current. The lifeguard began to check John, stopping at times to ask the crowd gathering to spread out. As I treaded water, I could feel my entire body weakening. All attempts were becoming confusing to me, as if my arms and legs no longer received any signals from my brain. I tried to yell. I tried to wave my arms for anyone to see me. Each time I came up for air, I watched the shoreline blur into a miniature version of what I knew to be the shoreline.

Another wave crashed on top of me. I came up for air. I went under again. I could feel my breathing start to slow. Hours away in Norfolk, Rica lay in the ICU, the tracheotomy tube coiled like something oceanic, and here I was, barely seventy pounds, being tossed toward unconsciousness. It wasn't that I wanted to sleep, but I remember thinking, *okay, okay, okay*, as if I were trying to convince some other part of myself. There was no more water, no gagging from its sharpness in my throat. No more stabbing pains in my stomach. The voice saying *okay* over and over was no longer my own.

That's when I knew.

What happened next is itself a blur in the myth of who I have become. I only remember being held. My neck cradled in someone's arm. It turns out the lifeguard who saved me was tethered to a chain of people who had held hands so that the one on the end would not be swept away. No sooner had I thought I was dead, than I realized I was going to live. Then there was the sky.

It seemed so small. What I could make of it. The waves occasionally slapped me in the face like a frustrated parent, or more like one who had been so scared, her reaction was to slap out of fear. I could understand that kind of fear forcing you to do things you wouldn't normally do.

Sleep

A week later I would start seventh grade at Great Bridge Junior High. The building had actually been the high school building from the year before. The new one was down the road on Hanbury, the one Rica would have graduated from. As I walked the hall-ways of my new school, I couldn't help but wonder which of these lockers had belonged to my sisters. I would have given anything to know. In which shadowy corner had each of them kissed their boyfriends, whispered plans to skip, or just meet up with friends after school.

The other kids all knew each other, had all gone to school together at the feeder school Southeastern Elementary. I was the *new* kid. But it was worse; whenever I started class, the teacher would say my name and pause and then ask, Isn't your sister one of the girls who — ? I would nod before they could finish, before they would suddenly express concern with their eyes. I would look away and then back at them to see if they had moved on, and if they were still studying my face, I would smile weakly, shrug until they would become aware they were staring.

The other kids in class were mostly oblivious, though a few who had older siblings would tell me, *Yeah, my sister knew your sister* or *Yeah, my brother knew her.* That was supposed to mean that we were linked together somehow, in the way small towns worked hard to foster a social hierarchy, our destinies predetermined by those in our family who had come before us. My problem within this fate was that a story of tragedy preceded me wherever I went.

If I met someone's parents, the mothers would inevitably tilt their heads to the side, almost appearing to pout before they would ask in a quiet voice, How is she? I would pause, because at first, I would think they meant my mother, or even my sister Tinah. I wouldn't think they were talking about Rica, who had only recently come out of the coma. What could I say other than She's fine, which was more to keep them from going further in their questioning? No one really wanted to know, I was convinced.

I suppose there were a few, but even then, out of consideration, I didn't want to pass along the burden that came with knowing. So instead of saying, She's not my sister anymore, I would say, She's good. I wouldn't say, My sister *died* at the scene of the accident. I wouldn't say, Her body was replaced with this body that doesn't function. I would say, I think she's doing fine, or We're hoping for the best. Just once I would love to say nothing and impersonate Rica in that moment.

To say nothing would describe her new life. She lies in a hospital bed, and people come into her room at all times to hook up and unhook things. Once, when she was still in a coma, the door to her hospital room was wide open, and we found a teenage boy standing next to her. The sheet covering Rica was lifted up so that he could gaze down at her naked body, so that he could stare at her hair. Equally stunned to discover us, he ran out of the room. It was only after he had left that the evil of that moment had settled into our understanding. I would love to have those seconds back.

The day before Thanksgiving, we brought her home from the hospital. Our church delivered a dinner to us the next day. Packed in deep Styrofoam containers, large portions of turkey and stuffing, the matted finish of cranberry sauce sliced from the can, all of it rested inside, drizzled with gravy. Our mother cut up the food in such small pieces that it could have been blended. Between sloppy chews, Rica slurped ginger ale from a messy straw. Is that good? our mother would say, nodding as if to prompt a positive response from Rica. Rica would only cough.

She was having trouble chewing, and any fluid she tried to take in had to first become a labored gurgling sound before she could swallow. Is it good? our mother would ask and run a hand through the short patch of hair that now buffered the scar. The boys from the neighborhood had stopped by when we first struggled to get her inside. She was a spectacle, another girl to gaze on. As for me, we couldn't get her in the house fast enough. She was my sister, and of course, I wanted her to get better, thought she would get better, but I also wished there were a way to hide her for a while, as if she might wrap herself within a cocoon and emerge to our surprise fully healed and hovering.

Boo, our mother said, still feeding Rica her Thanksgiving dinner. *Get your sister some more drink.*

I opened the lid of the dented Styrofoam cup and found tiny chunks floating in the yellowish liquid. The first time, I poured out everything, cleaning it. I refilled the cup with ginger ale and fresh ice. As the weeks became months and on, if I refilled her cup, the old was mixed with the new.

◗

When Rica first came home, she shared a room with Tinah. Nights, when it was late and everyone else was trying to sleep, Rica would rap her knuckles against a headboard or she would tap at the railing of her hospital bed — *ding, ding, ding* — as if her knuckle were the tongue in a bell. She wanted nothing more than to get Tinah's attention.

What, Rica, what? Tinah said, turning on the light. It had been going on this way.

Listen, Rica said, signing. She could do so — signing — because she still remembered the various contortions for the alphabet. We all did. Having had a cousin who lost her hearing as a toddler, we had years before learned the basics so that we could talk with our cousin. When Rica had awoken from her coma, ironically, she used sign language to tell us she was still *here*.

It's late, Tinah said. Go to sleep, okay? You can tell me in the morning.

No, Rica said. I want to tell you something now.

I want to tell you something too, but I won't, Tinah said and started to reach for the light switch.

Rica banged the handrail again, but it didn't matter, Tinah turned out the light. Rica tried to speak, but her words were mostly malformed breaths. Then silence.

Ding, ding, ding.

Tinah didn't reach for the light.

Ding, ding, ding.

Rica, go to sleep.

Ding, ding, ding.

I'm serious, go to sleep.

Ding, ding, ding.

What? What is it?

Ding, ding, ding.

What the hell? What? The light switched on.

Rica was smirking, giving both a cheesy grin and the bird at the same time. Fuh, she said. Fuh!

Fuck you too! Tinah said, pausing. They were both smiling. Then Tinah turned off the light.

Great Bridge

Our mother pushed her, and my brothers ran around the store. Or I would push Rica, and my brothers would still run around the store. Whichever store we happened to be in. It didn't matter. People were going to stare no matter what we did.

We could none of us say a word and listen to everything our mother said, and still people would stop what they were doing and watch us. If we were in a restaurant, children would watch intently while their parents would get nervous and point at something less interesting. The children would only turn away once they realized Rica wasn't going to vanish. This slouched figure frumpy in sweats would cough whenever she sipped through a straw and would cough whenever she took another bite of food.

Rica would get depressed about going out in public. She didn't want people to stare at her. Nights, Tinah would talk to her, and Rica would only sigh. This was in the beginning, after she had seen herself in the mirror and had to keep seeing this same self in the mirror. All those times she had spent getting ready before school, telling Tinah to wait just another minute before the two rushed off to make it to class in time, the vanity and the frustrations were only ghosts in the house now. As were the songs both she and Tinah had practiced on the piano in the living room. The long history of wrong notes. Ghosts.

This Same Expression

If Rica was especially quiet, I would ask, What's wrong? And when she wouldn't answer, I would know the answer. We all knew, in some ways, the same answer. Her face would take on the soft expression of someone resigned to a task. I had seen our mother bear this same expression. It involved looking at the present tense as something of a burden itself, an obstacle. So long as the present tense existed, their dreams remained unfulfilled.

◑

Halfway through my seventh-grade year, though, I found things were better than I had believed them initially to be. I made friends and even had a few reprieves sleeping over at other kids' houses. After school my mother would pick me up. I would stand at the end of the corridor, near the band room, and my mother's car would pull up in the fire lane, and there would be kids waiting on the sidewalk for their rides. They would all see Rica leaning her head against the glass, a dazed look on her broken face. Sometimes she even waved.

Once the doors to the school swung open, most of the kids hanging about would turn around to see me walking with my head down or in a quickened pace. If I could have dove into the backseat, so that no one really had a chance to see me, I would have. I would have done just that. Our mother would ask me how my day was, and

I would motion with my hands. Can't we just *go*? I would say, and our mother would just look at me, and I would peer back through the rear windshield. Those kids would already be gathering into a group to discuss what they had just seen, some stepping aside to gesture oddly with bent arms like they were retarded.

The Object of My Affection

We used to have burnt sienna shag carpet throughout our living room, where there was a cabinet with glass doors. In the hallway a portrait of Jesus pointing to his blue thorn-crown-enclosed heart hung with woven interlocking triangles of palm wedged into a corner of the portrait's frame. Our father had woven the palm years before.

Within the menagerie, Madame Alexander dolls rested on its mirrored bottom shelf. One in particular wore a blue checkered print dress. She had dark hair and an airbrushed pink cloud on each of her porcelain cheeks. Her name was Pussycat. Our mother had bought her especially for Rica, because Rica shared our mother's interest in playing with and preserving dolls. She liked to keep them on display.

On higher shelves of the cabinet, the glazed svelte Lladro figurines our father had brought back from Spain bore a resemblance, though less emaciated, to the poor angular figures in a Goya painting. Each statuette echoed some domestic scene. A mother holding a child. Two children at play on a teeter totter, suspended in their joy above a semicircle of plump Hummels singing wide-eyed in winter attire, the implication of pending snow from the artist's inclusion of orange scarves and tweed coats and wool caps. On other shelves were wooden carvings of angels. Preserved, too, was the Tonto doll I'd played with as a boy. That one, and a Geronimo.

When Rica first came home, it was difficult pushing her chair from room to room. The gray rubber wheels, especially the smaller ones, would catch and drag on the deep shag carpet. Sometimes the carpet would buckle and resemble a small swell, the wave of cloth then smoothing back to a flatness once you forced her chair forward and continued on with rolling her into the kitchen. Once you reached the kitchen, it all was easier. For this, our mother would have the carpet pulled up and replaced with linoleum so moves from room to room were seamless.

III.

The Unknowable Future

I was ambitious my eighth-grade year. Even before joining the wrestling team in late fall, I asked my mother in early August if I could sign up for football. I had never played organized ball before. My only football experience had been that of the late evening games in my neighborhood. In those games, we played in the invisible stadiums packed with hunched mosquitoes. The plays we called were mostly the cursing we tried out on each other, the trash talk and the swagger of boys trying to be men.

We loved to run into the shadows of makeshift end zones. We loved to hit late and leap over one another and sometimes make each other cry, especially if it happened to be one who would go home sulking. It made it better for some reason, burning in their mouths the curses they would save for another game.

My first real team was called the Bills, with the same insignia as Buffalo's NFL team. We had bright white jerseys with thick painted blue numbers on the chests and triple bands of red around the sleeves that hung past our growing, but measly, biceps. These were clean new uniforms, and had I known any better, I would have been a little more apprehensive about playing my first season.

With the opening game and each game afterward, we were crushed, *our asses handed to us,* some of us would joke when the coaches weren't around. We had a few good players, I suppose, but I wasn't one of them. I was just learning how to adjust to a game that seemed at the time to be more about premonition than skill. For one thing, I noticed I couldn't see ahead to make the right play. My time on the field was mostly a series of blurs — my heart in my throat, or my eyes burning from sweat dripping down. I remember only being skittish on defense. I was like a cat with socks tied to its paws. I bounced mindlessly around the field and only wanted to get out of the way of myself.

Before the plays, I would look to the sidelines, and there would be my sister sitting in her wheelchair, her head leaning to the side. My mother would be trying to raise my sister's hand in a cheer. Other families would be next to them while my brothers played tag in the background near one of the lift poles, an apron of light draped around them. It wasn't enough that this team I was now a part of lost every game. I felt cursed. Especially with my sister there, at times slumped over. A physical reminder that my family was cursed as well.

I could look up from a play, maybe I had assisted in a tackle, and Rica would be there in the same spot, on the sideline, staring not at me and not at the field. I didn't know where she was staring, or if she could even really see me. Our mother would be clapping her hands against my sister's hands, even the one that was curved and had to be strapped with Velcro in a plastic brace. Their joy would only add to the embarrassment I felt for myself and for those who cheered for me.

My shirt wouldn't be tucked in anymore. It would be full of fresh grass stains and some blood. The tail would sway below my waist and would look more like a skirt around my thin padded legs. To say I was of normal size would have distorted the comparison. I was a shrimp, tiny, hardly comprising a good spit. I must have looked somewhat comical running around the other boys, who were taller by at least a foot. After the games I would shuffle my way over to my mother, who had already started the work of pushing Rica back to the car.

That was good, my mother would always say, like she had just attended a piano recital. That was nice. She could have been talking about anything.

Games where I had no tackles: *That was good.*

Games where I, by sheer luck, blocked a punt or sacked the quarterback: *That was nice.*

My mother had other things on her mind, though.

The entire season wasn't always glum. Something happened. And it wasn't just the little skull and crossbones stickers our coaches started handing out for tackles either. Halfway through the season, I felt the game click in my head. Just enough for me to breathe and settle down in the mix of bodies and start making some tackles. I was horrible on offense, yes, had tried it out and was just plain horrible. In practice I had been leveled and lost my breath and had to spend a few plays out just to keep from tearing up again.

On defense, however, it was different. There was no pressure to move anything forward, no pressure to hold onto the ball. There was only the love for chaos and the embrace of forcing anyone unlucky enough to be carrying the ball down to the hard, cold field. The first time I made a solo tackle, I had been so stunned by it that I hit the kid again before he got to his feet. I was lucky the referee didn't catch it. But I did. I was hungry for it to happen again. I wanted to put him in the ground.

Despite finishing our regular season with a perfect losing record, the off-season bowl game gave us one more opportunity to prove ourselves. It was at this night game that we, as enthusiasts love to say, *showed up to play.* We outran, out tackled, and outscored the other team. We didn't look like a group of kids that had just spent months on a diet of humility. We were finally a team.

I know it was because of this season's exciting ending that I decided to play again the following year. Most of the others did the same. That following year, with the exception of a few new kids to the roster, we were essentially the same team we had been as the Bills; though our coaches, out of superstition, renamed us the Cardinals, a team they had coached some years before to league victory. I didn't blame them. Sometimes change was what you needed. Instead of losing every game in the regular season, the reborn Cardinals ended up winning every one.

Brutal Pupil

It could say, You and your family will make it through this.

At the same time it said, Of course, you will die.

The first time I saw the pupil, I believed every word. My sister Rica would try to swing her head, and that brutal pupil of hers, the eye on the side that was paralyzed, the pupil seemed to spread wider. As if inviting the surrounding light to disappear inside it.

Go ahead, it seemed to say, *get lost.*

So I did.

Now my mother is asking me to help her get Rica out of the car and into the house. This feat involves a series of moves, a strategizing that my mother has mastered since my sister has come home from the hospital. Moving my sister around is a chore my mother endures without question or resentment. If anything, my mother is pleasant in the way she undertakes what has become for her routine. If anything, it is almost inhuman.

Sometimes I get quiet in their presence, as I do now, and my mother simply looks at me. Not in a reprimanding way, nor does she allow for any pity, whether from her or for her.

Help me with your sister, is what she says.

I open the car door and immediately smell the sharp, bitter stench to which I am already growing accustomed. I lift my sister's feet off of the floorboard and position them just so. Her calves are moist to the touch. This makes my stomach turn. I want to gag, but I know if I do, I will offend her.

She is starting to slide slowly onto her side. The emergency brake is already digging into her ribs. Standing up quickly I grab her under both arms and pull her to me. She could be one of our father's duffel bags filled with clothes.

Buh . . . buh, she says, the word never fully forming on her lips.

Stand her up, our mother says. I try. I step in and shift my hips. Now that I'm on the wrestling team, I think about the hip toss, any other move for gaining leverage on your opponent. But I'm also barely eighty pounds. I don't know if I can move her without my mother helping me some. She outweighs me by at least sixty pounds, if not more.

I don't know if I have what it takes to hold onto her.

◗

It spoke to me.

Who will you let tell your story?

I didn't answer, afraid of what I'd admit.

Outside, Glen, Timmy, and the others were kicking up dust in an empty field where some of the older kids sometimes rode their dirt bikes, launched airs from one dirt clod mound to the next, each mound tamped down with tread, sprigs of weeds leveled. I could hear my friends yelling, cussing up storms in the warm evening.

I stared out the window screen and then back to Rica. Back to the pupil that had a say in both of our lives. Why are you still here? it said.

Because Mom took the boys up to the store to get dinner, and Tinah's still at work.

I watched Rica's mouth. Oh, she mouthed, but no sound. Outside, the boys were colliding. Looking back, I think of James

Wright's poem of the high school players in the stadium, galloping across the torn football field, wrecking one another.

Do you wish you were dead? I said out of the blue.

She smiled. She signed *No* with her good hand, but kept smiling, as if I should understand. I watched her smile. I searched her face for the sister I once knew, but she wasn't really there. I found, instead, the downy black hairs fuzzed above her lip.

The hair was a side effect of the medications she took. And her smooth skin, the light tan complexion that rarely held blemishes, it was no longer smooth but blotched now. As if a burn had grafted itself to her cheeks and would allow no part of her face to be consistent in tone. Even her eyebrows mocked the ghost of who she had been, leaving little chance that a stranger might see her for the first time and find any trace of the meticulous care she had once been able to take in herself.

Our mother, of course, took her to beauty salons, and sometimes our cousin Judy, who had once been trained in hair and makeup, would come to the house. People cared for her, but it was different now. Each hairstyle was a version of what someone else wanted. Their intentions were good, but even if they asked afterward if she liked it, it was always afterward. She never had a true say in what direction they would take, my sister who just the year before would cut out pictures of models from issues of *Cosmo* and tape them to her mirror.

I went to the dresser drawer, dipped a cotton swab into the frosted plastic container of Vaseline. I spread it over her chafed lips. *Buh*, she said, *buh*.

It's okay, I said. I could smell her now. I wanted to let her know it was okay. Mom will be home soon, I said. I don't know why, but I sat there next to her with my eyes closed. I'd seen my mother do this countless times, as if she were a monk meditating. I opened my eyes when I felt her hand squeeze mine.

What are you doing? I said.

She was taking my hand and trying to put it between her legs.

Stop it, I said. I know. Mom will be home soon. Just wait.

She smiled again, especially because I was standing up now.

I can't change you, I said.

With her hand, she signed *Yes*.

No, I can't, I said.

Yes.

No.

Yes.

I can't!

Yes. As she signed this, she smiled, though this time, it seemed menacing to keep responding this way, like she was trying to play a trick on me. Her eyebrows, those whiskered curves constricted, furrowing.

What? I said.

Her face suddenly went soft and with it, all of my anger diminished.

What? I whispered, but she didn't look at me.

Both eyes were closed and her head fell back, along with her limbs, not just the unstable side. She began to shudder like siding on an old farmhouse, a storm blowing through and causing random things alongside to creak.

Rica, I said, but I knew even as I said her name she wouldn't respond. I had seen this before and ran to the kitchen for one of the big spoons. I had to force it into her mouth, her yellowed teeth clamped, chattering now against the metal stem of the spoon, against the concave head I pressed against the tongue.

Rica, I said again and stroked her hair as her body shivered below me. Like the older sibling, already gone to where I, the younger one, couldn't follow.

Here was the same sister who had taken baths with me when I was not yet five. I still remember those evenings. She would run her finger through the foam lather that lay across my back like a thin cape. She would say, *What letter is this?* I would stare ahead at the new silver faucet of the tub. It was our new house in Chesapeake, our family having moved here from base housing in Norfolk. I would concentrate on what I thought was being written. I usually guessed wrong. Sometimes, just to hear her laugh. Sometimes, because it was silly, and she was with me. I suppose, even then, I was aware that I loved her.

On those nights, our father gone on deployment, I could hear our mother in the hallway whistling *Que Sera, Sera,* as she was putting up the folded clothes into the closet. It is a tune that haunts me to this day. Only later would I discover it was featured in Hitchcock's *The Man Who Knew Too Much.* With the melody still hanging in the air, I could hear Tinah calling from the other side of the house, and I knew I wasn't just a boy, with nothing expected of me. I remember believing I was the man of the house. I actually believed it.

Almost Morning

I never knew where our mother went exactly, only that some nights I would stay up and it would be almost morning before I would hear her car pull into the driveway. The first few times it happened, I would be angry, having waited up for her. I would suspect she had been drinking, but I would never ask her directly. Instead, I would lie on the couch and feign sleep, my face pressed deep into the pillow I'd brought from my bed, my younger brothers in the next room filling the house with their even breathing.

Our mother would enter the quiet and head straight for the TV. I would open my eyes slightly, just in time to see her rest a palm on the set. Feeling its warmth, testing whether or not it's been on for long. Without turning around, she would say to me, You should be asleep.

I was scared, I would say, even though I had learned that fear in her children usually sets her off.

What's there to be scared of? she would answer. I couldn't tell her it was because I was only twelve and all night I thought I heard noises. That I was worried something might happen to my younger brothers asleep in the next room. I knew she would tell me stories about the farm in North Carolina and about having to watch her sister's children. How at ten years old, just a girl, she had been given away to an aunt in Virginia and told to live in this woman's house until her parents sent for her, which happened to be three

years later. You couldn't tell our mother something, especially in
matters of hardship, without having her draw comparisons to her
own troubled life. If you happened to be one of her children, your
grievances were usually dismissed. Life was not *that* bad.

It was for this last reason that I refrained from explaining. I
had trouble sleeping, especially with Rica having recently been
moved to Fishersville, a rehabilitation center nestled on the other
side of Virginia near the Shenandoah Valley. I was worried that
something else might happen. Every time I visited her with our
mother, Rica seemed more helpless, an infant but worse, an infant
that had finished developing. Despite our canned responses whenever anyone might mention the future — that dream of her walking
and talking again — we were starting to wonder if she would ever
progress beyond lying in a hospital bed and staring at the wall, or
staring at the few cards taped to the wall.

After a long stay at Fishersville, Rica would eventually come
home. There would be nurses who would visit the house and
help our mother with providing care. Sometimes there would be
stretches of no help, and our mother would forgo employment
to be at home so that Rica could see her. But then it was back to
Fishersville again for more extended cycles of physical therapy.
Traveling to and from the rehab center took roughly seven hours,
if you drove the speed limit, and for a period of time, our mother
would make that trip every other day, all while trying to balance
the needs of her other children.

Come morning, after those nights of our mother going out, I
wanted to tell her I worried that even she might not come home
again. I knew she was bearing a burden I would never fully understand. She blamed herself for having let Rica go with her friend
Ellen. She didn't have to come out and say it. It was obvious. I
had never met Ellen's mother, but I imagined she was suffering
as well. She had to be. We could at least still touch Rica. Ellen, on
the hand, was gone entirely.

The Other Boy

My teammates call the easy ones *fish*. It has stuck with me. Fish. As strange as it is to admit, I understand these fish for this reason. Fish become the other boys who become the fish. Their suffering is always circular. Now I held this one's body in my hands and counted the hinged breaths.

Watching this boy struggle out of water, you would think he was doing everything in his power to stay alive. You would almost laugh, but then not laugh. It would be funny. You might laugh. He makes faces without meaning to make faces. His cheeks bloated, his bottom lip drooping like the foot of a clam. Then he might pull it together briefly, his cheeks returning to normal, his lip straightening a bit. In those moments he would almost look human were it not for his eyes now yellowing, beyond jaundiced, the way they bulge with smeared vessels around the edges. The eyes themselves become things to poke with a stick and watch the fluid inside finally release, spilling over the wrestling mat.

The other boy continues to flop around.

I am there on the mat.

I am not there on the mat. I scoot closer to the fish and listen to its labored breathing, the way some nights I sneak into my sister's room and reach through the brushed silver bars of her hospital bed. There would be no one nearby, and I would put a hand on her chest.

Even though I am thirteen, her breasts would not be breasts.

I wouldn't worry that I was touching my older sister in this way. It wouldn't be in any way other than the way it should be: a brother checking on his sister to see if she was still breathing. A brother touching his sister to find out. Even when I knew she was asleep, I would sometimes say, *Are you still alive?* There would be no response.

Then again: Are you still alive?

I wait for her chest to rise, and it feels like a swell in the surface of her breath. Then it will fall to shuddering, like a wave in the ocean. A part of it breaks before it actually reaches the shore. Of course I knew she was alive, but I wanted to delay what I already knew. In this way life seems only a series of willed misunderstandings. You do this to get by.

I pretended. It is difficult to think of her throughout the day. Her going day in and day out like she does, as she has had to do now that she is unable to walk or to talk.

Her breathing is nothing like the ocean. Even an erratic one, a wave would seem too controlled, especially the ones that approach the shore in sets, glassy and spaced apart. So much so that you could fool yourself, think there was someone else controlling the interval of each wave's arrival. A magician, maybe. Or a god teaching patience.

Are you still alive?

No, her breathing would be erratic. It is more labored, like the ocean, yes, but only when the wind is blowing northeast and the surface of the water looks choppy. Like a washing machine.

For the sound of her breathing, too, was like the end of a curtain against the screen in an open window. As if a gust from far

off arrived to force cloth against metal, cloth to brush the metal
screen over and again. Enough of this and the cloth will fray.

◗

I pull myself closer to the fish. At one point, I am the fish, and then
I'm not the fish. I want to put my hand on its chest, but the fish
jerks back and stares at me. I feel my own heart jolt, as if suddenly
colder, like a fish's heart. In that moment of communion, I might
change into something else. I try to settle the fish down.

If I can settle it down, I think, maybe it will become a boy again.
Sometimes all it takes is for one to believe you are this thing, and
then you can become whatever it is you believe. If you want to
win, then you imagine yourself doing so before it happens. This
is the boy in me who has only faith to lose. It makes sense, and
then doesn't make sense.

It barely makes sense. I know this. I know, but I decide to take
the fish into my arms and hold its wet throat. I study close its chin.
The tiny whiskers surprise me most. When I study its eyes again,
I find they are still yellow, no longer bloodshot. Its mouth opens
and closes, mimicking the way a boy might breathe if he were a
boy and trying to breathe.

If you smelled his breath, you would think of cut bait, of dried
guts found on the blade of a pocketknife. You might even think of
things washed up on the shore near Little Island, the remote section
of Virginia Beach bordering Back Bay Wildlife Refuge. Along this
stretch of coastline would be randomly relevant things. Mottled
bodies of pelicans throttling the air before lifting off, or sandpipers
zigzagging on the ground, toying with the shore break that never
reaches their tiny legs. This brief world would be covered, instead,
with the clear, sticky film of brine, for the ocean wind would be
more salt than air. Nothing would be wholly itself.

Everyone in the moment seems intent for something to happen
to at least one of us. How can we disappoint them? Thinking of

Rica sitting in her wheelchair at home, I want now to only hold longer the body that resists my full grasp. I try harder to move the body into position, to tilt it and expose its back. I want to break the plane of the 45-degree angle, but the body resists again.

I smile. I can't help it. I smile because I know I'm not concentrating hard enough, and if the fish eludes my grasp, it might try sliding its way across the gymnasium floor and out onto the freshly mown grass. Down the prickled embankment that feeds into the nearby creek that feeds into the Albemarle Canal.

You're dead, I say, and when the fish stares back at me, as if in recognition, I only say it again to convince us both.

No matter what I say, or even how many times I will say it, the struggle continues. It has to continue, and that's fine. I put my knee near his kidney and drive it in slowly so the referee won't catch it and caution me. I want it all to be over, but I also know that if I want it bad enough, it will be over, it would have already been over. I don't want it bad enough. I hate the fish for this lesson it teaches me. I hate its pale flesh, the newly reddening rims of its eyes.

I hate its pathetic mouth pretending to take in air when I know it isn't really taking in air. I am through with pretending, even though it has been easy for this boy to become something else and stay that way. This boy is a boy who never had a chance to be a boy. I understand this.

I pull the fish to me. I press hard my chest to rest on this chest. Again, the body is too slippery and twists away momentarily, but I pull it back by its fake arms. They are flimsy limbs that do nothing useful except give me something to bar my arm against and leverage another tilt. Though if I bend them in the opposite direction, the fish will flail.

I make the fish flail.

We finally shift out of bounds, and after tying up again, I make sure to sweep the legs that aren't really legs at all. I am quick, but not especially quick. The other boy, after all, is just a fish. I chase him. I pull him down into the watery mat.

Since they aren't really legs, it isn't going to hurt if I bury an elbow into these legs. It won't pain the fish if I wedge my knee against a hamstring that isn't really a hamstring and with my free arm dig an elbow into the spine that isn't really a spine. The fish flails again.

I spot my mother sitting in the bleachers. Her hands are clasped. She won't smile. I want to lift the fish and show her, but only her. I want to carry it outside and release it back into the waters of our shared memory. Yet, I want it to stay. I want it to become a boy again.

I wanted to become a boy again, to go back and start over. Before the referee blew the whistle. Before we nodded at one another and quickly shook hands. Before we ran to the inner circle of the mat and placed our feet on the colored tape marking our starting position. Before we took off our sweats and put on our headgear. Before even the crowd arrived.

Before the summer and the school year and the summer before the accident.

Yes, before *that* June. The world would hardly be perfect, as it always would be, but in it, there would at least be this girl. And she could talk. And she could tell you what she wanted to become. And it wouldn't seem like a dream, because she would be the one asking you questions, and just by answering, you would be telling her you were alive.

Suspension of Disbelief

There is the smell of each crumpled headgear, a blend of *patis*, fish sauce used in Filipino dishes, and dirty socks. The singlets, rarely washed, soak in the stale air forever hovering in the boys' locker room. No matter how vigilant the custodians are with clean mops and clear buckets of bleach water, there is no getting rid of this smell.

Piled in each locker are the lifeless sweatshirts and sweatpants worn through practices. Because these clothes are never washed, each item retains every dried stain, every blended scent. There are stains on stains. Moments dreamt of cheerleaders, of the girls from our homerooms. Their mouths found a way into our beds each night before sleep eventually crushed us. Sometimes we dreamt of teachers too. There was no discretion in who would come for us.

All were women who wanted one thing. And, of course, the older women knew more than the girls. It was how it had to be. In our minds, every adult wanted to be young again, and yet we knew that experience always dominated youth. What made the thought of these older women so alluring was that in these dreams, they lowered the shadows of their bodies into our corner of the world and we disappeared inside each and every one of them.

In the locker room I sit on the slab bench. Waiting near the exit door is the scale where the ghost of every wrestler before me stands and fiddles with the increments, shifting, searching for the *sweet spot*. It's where the scale's small silver-painted arm balances its one pointer within the plane. Every scale is different, the sweet spot harder to find in some, easier in others.

At seventy-four pounds I'm the first weight class on the team. I have to go first. Everyone is standing around. Coaches too. Arms folded and eyes watching only the one metal arm reaching to the one side, checking its distance against the next body. I strip down to my underwear, and the moment I step on the scale, the arm plunks to the top. I know this sound all too well. Everyone knows this sound. It is the sound of a forfeit.

My coach steps in and tells me to hurry up and get dressed, that the others can go on ahead and weigh in. This means there is work to be done. I reach into my gym bag and throw on my sweats. My teammates, eager to help, give me theirs as well. I don't care. I pile them on. Some are damp and cold from being damp. I feel like a sumo made of cloth. I try not to think of the stained sleeves, their smell the smell of pancake batter.

And the chests of these sweatshirts, the cloth doesn't give in some places. Spattered as they are like the asbestos ceiling tiles above with signs of water damage. I pile them on because it is time to weigh in. At seventy-four and one-half pounds, I'm overweight.

If I'm to qualify, I have no choice but to drop eight ounces in less than twenty minutes. Other starters have already begun to weigh in. Someone rushes me. I can barely turn my body from being layered in so many different shirts. I'm rushed down the hall, through the showers, and soon I find myself in what appears to be a vestibule, not unlike one I use on Sundays to change before serving as an altar boy. But this shadowy room, unlike the one at the church, consists of large canvas boxes. Each box is grimy; most are overturned. Chunky, lint-covered gray wheels braced below for the laundry they haul.

Someone says, *Crawl inside*, and so I do, and the box begins to move. I feel like a tiny ball hiding under a cup, like one in a magic trick. Follow the ball. Where's the ball? The steam coming from the radiator along the wall crawls under the box to be with me. For once, I welcome the smell it brings.

It is the smell of my making weight. This is only a small part of the dirty business of it, the necessary evil before so much glory is to be had. Pancake batter again mixed with the pungency of rust. I wonder if I'll get a certificate to frame. I wonder if it comes with a medal. How nice it would be to get a medal.

I would put it in her hand and listen to her try to say my name. And I would wear it to school and let girls touch it. I would want their fingertips, even the ones who bite their nails, to play with it.

If someone said, Why are you still wearing that? I would say, Shut up.

If someone said, Isn't it time you took it off? I would say, Who are you again?

I would add, Fuck off.

I would say, You're right. I'm being silly.

I would say, *Thank you, thank you, thank you.*

I crouch there in the dark. I can smell myself among the others. I imagine I'm only sitting inside the van, inside the old fort. I imagine I live only inside one of the photographs. I'm in the one car that's disappeared inside the naked woman. I'm in the car I can't see when I stare at the picture of this woman, because the car is deep and traveling in the dark.

If this were a movie, I would have been miniaturized to where I could drive the car farther inside her. I would turn on the headlights and continue on. Because it was Hollywood, the landscape of her body would be reduced to a series of easily identifiable objects. I would take part in the compartmentalization of the woman's interior. I would be a falsehood among a falsehood.

I would be there in the car, in the suspension of disbelief, turning on the headlights that were not real and then switching on the bright lights in hopes of discovering something from which to draw a comparison within my own boyish fears. And because it would be a movie, our beautiful make-believe world would have the beginnings of a fetus suspended like a bunch of grapes, but here it is above the car just as the car suddenly stalls. I would wipe the fog of my breath off the inside of the windshield.

I would blink my eyes and step out into the womb that would be lit like aurora borealis and looking heavenly and, for being so, wholly unbelievable. And as a twist, one that would make the cynical viewer say under their breath, No *fucking* way, I would see the fetus was no longer a fetus. It would already be a baby, clean and bloodless, and I would recognize its face, and I would wait for it to grow up and become me so that one of us could finally disappear.

Under the box I feel the sweat gather inside my nose and then drip to my chin. I have a nose like my father. A true Filipino nose. Flat. I wonder how much my nose weighs. More than eight ounces, I'm sure of it. A flat nose weighs a lot, I think. I pinch it between my fingers, which are starting to prune. If my nose were a thin, straight nose, I wouldn't be where I was, under an overturned laundry cart. My body would not be layered with the soiled dreams of my teammates. I wouldn't have eight ounces to lose. My nose would be thin and straight and I would be eight ounces lighter for sure.

All I want to do is make weight. That's it. Then I can settle down with my bag of food. Some call theirs their *stash* or their *booty*, like they were pirates. Like they had robbed for what they had now earned the right to consume. The others have their bags of food with them and are scattered in the gymnasium, huddled in corners. They are enjoying it all, and I have no choice but to wait.

I know the ritual. Weigh in, then drink, eat whatever you want.

At the junior high level, you didn't know any better. There is no science to it, not like there is once you compete in high school and on. Some, though, are careless and gorge on the giant chocolate chip cookies. The cookies are mostly wet globs of dough wrapped in wax paper, saved from the school cafeteria. Others eat sub sandwiches piled with salami or pastrami or both and wash them down with piss-colored Gatorade or Big Gulp cups filled with Mountain Dew, also the color of piss.

As for my stash, I can almost taste the double-decker peanut butter and honey sandwich I'd made in reverence earlier that morning. My solemn gestures had been those of a priest's, preparing the Eucharist for consumption by all, instead of those of a growing boy staving off the jitters of his hunger long enough to wield a butter knife and refasten the bread bag, screw back on the blue plastic top. Eating was something to treasure.

It is sweltering under the cart. I suddenly wonder if they have forgotten about me. I wipe my face. Someone will remember, I tell myself. I am, after all, the first wrestler to start things off. Today is the city tournament. The day the others and I have waited for all season. It is a chance to win an individual title. It is a chance to gain recognition within the school. Cheerleaders who waited patiently at the edge of the mat will have their own chance to jump up and kick their slender legs in the air and say your name at the same time they smile and scream. It is a memory of joy you want for them.

But first, there is the scale. I have to face my own weight before I face anyone else. What would my father think of me were he able to see me now? I wonder. And what about my mother, at home taking care of my sister, how each day is spent repositioning Rica's body in bed, or lifting her up and guiding her into the wheelchair. What would my mother think if she could see me wrapped in sweats and curled under the heated dark of a laundry cart? I am a tiny ball no one has been able to find. I am the driver of the car.

I know there are more important things than making weight. Yet, how nice it would be to make weight and then wrestle and then win. How nice it would be to see the girl you had a crush on lift green and gold pom-poms in the air and yell your name in front of a crowd of strangers. How nice it would be to be normal. To be one of the boys who is just a boy and not one who some of the adults point to and say, *His sister was the one who . . .*

I decide the heat is making me delusional. But before I can stand up and throw off this cart, someone rushes in and does it for me. They find me shivering underneath. What's the matter? they say. They don't care, and for this, I'm grateful. They push a knotted jump rope into my hands. I have almost no time. My entire body is slick underneath, which is a good sign. The only spots for which I feel any of the gym's cooler air are my wrists. The sleeves keep sliding as I begin the constant ritual of jumping up and down. I start off slow and then run in place.

My hands exposed are like magnets for the cold air. They draw it against my skin. I want relief from the heat, but I also want to sweat. I know I need to sweat more than anything. That is the only way I will make weight. If I sweat, then I can lose a portion of myself. My face peeks from below a puffy red wool cap. I'm too intent to notice how the gym has begun to fill with people. Now I turn toward a corner near the pull-up bar, where earlier in the year I challenged the school record. It was nothing. I was so light, I only had to think of gripping the bar and my body would lift to where my chin cleared it entirely. How I'd love now to be hoisted simply by the thought of being hoisted.

Maybe I could stand on the scale and feel myself growing lighter with each thought. No. That would be craziness. I just needed more time. If I had at least an hour, I wouldn't worry. But I barely had a handful of minutes now. I tried to find a rhythm for the jump rope and the sphere around me it might maintain. The rope kept slapping the wood slats of the basketball court. I ran in place, sprinting within the sphere. I could feel my feet start to drag. It was hard to keep going with the weight of those shirts and pants, the wet heft of it all. I hold my breath and feel my heart in my neck.

My coach, a short stocky man with feathered brown hair and a slight waddle in hiked athletic shorts, steps out of the locker room door and smiles at me. I'm still jumping rope. You think you did it? Coach asks.

I don't know. I don't want to say too much just in case I'm over. I have always been too serious when I shouldn't be. As much as I can remember being so, pensive to a fault. It has only been heightened by Rica's accident, my need to ponder. I know it is a burden, and yet I know it's the furthest thing from a burden. It is my own weight, and one I should learn to live with if I'm to keep going.

When I approach the scale, I can't help wishing the small arm has been broken from so many others weighing in. This thought makes me smile. That would be a miracle, I think. And I needed one of those; that would be much needed right now.

Well, it's now or never, Coach says, unfolding his arms. He grips my shoulder, the way a father might in a gesture of pride for his son. My own father could not be there. I was sure I knew why, but at that moment, with Coach guiding me toward the scale, I had forgotten my father's excuse, if there even was one. I decide I have only to concentrate harder and I will be hoisted by the act of remembering.

Inside the locker room, they gather. It is dim, near evening, and the other coaches from the other schools stand with arms crossed in front of them. Elbows rest on the curved domes of their tight paunch bellies. Some even rock back on the heels of new running shoes.

C'mon, one says, twirling his hand in the air like there was something sticky on the end of it he wanted to get off.

Yeah, we haven't got all day, says another one, nudging the other coaches. They are laughing. They are excited to begin the tournament just as much as the boys themselves are excited to begin wrestling in it.

Each second is suddenly inescapable. Like all the clocks have every living person in a headlock. My sister, no doubt, could struggle to no end other than the one that held her and her voice in near silence. She is at home, I know, sitting in a wheelchair. Staring at the far side of a room.

I want to be different. I want it to be different, and at the same time, I feel the same hold. Each time I take a breath, the invisible arms tighten. If I'm not careful, my breath will leave me for good.

I strip down to my underwear. The fact that it clings to me front and back, I know it weighs more than it had earlier. That is a good thing and a bad thing. I step on the scale. The arm of it creeps to the top. It is going to stop, I tell myself. Please *stop.*

Then it begins easing down, back into range. I smile, exhausted before the tournament has even started. Where is my sandwich? Where is the endless stream from the water fountain? I don't care. I'll taste its rust.

But like so many things—

The arm begins to climb again. It climbs within the moment I find myself staring, waiting and watching for how this mindless piece of metal will wreck my life. I reposition my footing on the small piece of grip tape. It is a frayed piece pressed to a metal rectangular platform that slides like the deck of a skateboard. I'm good at skateboarding, having recently learned to drop in at Mount Trashmore. Trashmore is a park my mother has taken me to in nearby Virginia Beach. The skate ramp there boasts 1½ foot of vertical, 10½ foot by 10½ foot with quick transitions. Something like that.

But the slight slide on the scale is different. Instead of launching airs over the coping, I need to simply become air. To grow lighter. Instead of a front-side boneless, I just need for a moment to become boneless. Exploit any absence of my body. Grow lighter, I think to myself. Grow lighter.

And if I can't do that, I need to do what most wrestlers know to do, find the scale's sweet spot. Find the zone in which the undetectable resides. It comes from leaning your body slightly at an angle, just enough so that the scale forgives you a few ounces. That's all I need, just a few measly ounces.

I shift and lean. Someone said, Stop doing that.

No matter how hard I try, I can't find it. Hey, they say again. Cut it out.

At this point, I let out all my breath, as if to be free of even breath. My ribs become more pronounced over my splotchy skin, which is usually a light brown. I inhale slowly, and my throat tightens around the last breath. If I let it out slowly, perhaps only my soul would become tethered to it. Like a magician pulling free a long, colorful scarf from his sleeve, I could allow for my soul to leave in one slow flourish. In this way, I might unburden myself to make weight.

I let out another breath, but it is just a breath.

The scale's arm doesn't budge from its spot above the plane. Someone slaps me on the back. *Go ahead, and take 'em off,* they say. I look confused, though I know it has to be done. I let my underwear drop onto the floor. *Thwack.*

The underwear looks like a beached jellyfish, like it is dusted with sand.

There I stand, thirteen, but with no sign of maturity—no hair, nothing at all. Most of the others on my team have already begun to change. But not me. I'm still a boy. Any other time it would have been fine, but not now. Not like this. I shiver from the attention.

Standing on the scale, I cup myself, watch the arm drop slightly, but then rise again. It is teasing me. I let out more breath, but it doesn't seem to help. I don't need to breathe, I keep telling myself.

What I wouldn't give to make weight, to have this entire ordeal vanish quickly into the past. As far as I knew, no one stood between the title and me.

Raise your arms up, one of the coaches says. I didn't want to do that. I felt ridiculous already. Though the locker room is not air-conditioned and has no open windows, only small rectangles of translucent glass framed in chain links, despite all of this trapped heat, I continue to shiver.

Go on, someone says.

Stop being a pussy, one of the boys whispers.

Hey, don't say that, says one of the coaches, smiling.

I take a deep breath again. As I release it, I stretch my arms toward the ceiling. I don't watch the scale's arm, its tiny metal finger that controls my fate. Instead, I close my eyes and imagine myself as something else — a leaf in a storm, a grain of sand tumbling in the surf.

Birthmark

The coaches started their discussion — some saying, *He's made it, he's made it. Let's go, let's start this thing*! Others agreed, and hearing this, I opened my eyes and found that I was floating above the room. Could it be true? Someone should grab me by the ankle and pull me back down. I floated above them, and no one seemed to notice.

Wait, one of the coaches said. His arms crossed in front of his puffed-up chest. I remembered this coach, whose face was slightly disfigured, mottled, as if most of his face had been covered by a botched skin graft or even an unfortunate birthmark. Maybe it was from a horrible burn he'd suffered during childhood. I didn't know what it was from, though, had not given it any thought really. Not in the way the others from my team had made cracks about it. Kids, as everyone knows, can be cruel.

I had not thought about the mark until now, when this coach shook his head and said, simply, No, I don't think so. I had beaten one of his wrestlers earlier in the season. I remembered this and thought, at first, it was because of this fact that the coach had said what he'd said.

No, this man said again, I really don't think so.

I stepped off the scale and started to put on my clothes. Each item felt damper than the last one I touched, which just moments ago had clung to me like a starfish. I looked at the man still crossing his arms in front of himself. Sitting on a concrete slab, shivering, I glanced up and studied with vehemence the man's face.

Had the disfiguration been a continent on a globe, like those found in geography classes, it would have been the size of Australia. Like Australia, so much of it would have been uninhabitable, filled with the world's most poisonous snakes. But I liked Australia. It was the land of celebrated surfers, of the pop band Men At Work (though I had long stopped listening to them), of *Mad Max* and *The Road Warrior.*

I didn't want the birthmark to be Australia. I didn't want this man's face to be a place that exotic. I decided it would be easy to hate a face such as his. But, in truth, I couldn't. Through Rica I had recently witnessed the hard lesson of disfigurement. Despite her appearance, she was still who she was.

I thought again of that first time at the hospital. No one stopped me walking through the doors of the ICU, not until it was too late. I saw her lying there, her face bruised, her neck swollen beneath the blue snake. The sister I had known was now dead, and here she was in a different form, newly born but broken. But maybe, too, this coach with his marked face was only casting a vote for integrity, for I thought I had glimpsed the scale's arm drop only briefly and break the plane but then begin its ascent. I couldn't really say. Even though the other coaches were in agreement, I knew the decision needed to be a consensus. Otherwise, I suppose, this man thought the boy before him might grow up feeling corners could be cut. That life could sometimes be fair, even when it really had no good reason to be.

Hello Again

If you lived in Great Bridge during the mid-1980s, you would have seen her. I'm sure of it. At one of the stoplights, at least once.

She would have been the girl slouched in the passenger's seat of a white Nissan Sentra. Her head would be pressed against the glass. Her thick, unruly black hair spidering out like a broken aura. She would have been the girl you might have wondered what, exactly, was wrong with her. That is, if you'd recently moved to this town.

Otherwise, you would have known a few of the details: On June 14, 1983, in Southern Shores, North Carolina, a dump truck loaded with sand had slammed into a Datsun filled with four teenagers. The driver, a sixteen-year-old who'd only recently received her license, had died at the scene. The others in the car would be flown to Norfolk General, where one would die, and the other two, both comatose, would emerge changed forever.

◖

In stores, people would gawk. They would, of course, be studying her, and they, especially older women, would feel the need to touch her hand and say, Hello, *dear*. Rica would sign, Hello, to them, and they would nod and smile, nod and smile, and I would think to myself, You've got to be fucking kidding me, and these women would tell her how pretty she was, and again, I would think, You've got to be fucking kidding me.

Rica would lift her head and bare her crooked smile, and if they looked closely, they would see pieces of her front teeth that appeared glued back on, glazed at the point of repair. Anyone in their right mind would know she was hideous, but those women would keep on smiling back at Rica.

They would ask our mother how she was, and Rica would raise her hand and sign, *I see God, and you will all be dead*. Our mother would touch Rica's hand and not translate. Rica, she would say quietly, stop that. These women would ask, What's that, dear? And I would want more than anything to spell out the letters to them, because what my sister was saying was the truth, but no one seemed to want to hear it, except for me.

Flat Bottom

The transitions were too tight.

They forced each of us who dropped in to quickly adjust to the minimal flat bottom. Once you had recovered from the steep descent, then you would begin the immediate ascent up the other side. It was a smaller half pipe than the sky blue ramp at Trashmore, the park in Virginia Beach that had once been a giant landfill off of I-44. All of us who had ridden our boards over from the junior high had spent the year before practicing at the well-known skatepark, their two ramps affectionately dubbed *Little Trash* and *Big Trash* by the locals, which we weren't.

But here at this ramp, we felt empowered by our past. All of us had some experience skating *vert*. I don't remember if this new ramp had any vertical, maybe a few inches near the coping. I had learned to fifty-fifty, as well as rock-n-roll, and was eager try out these two basic tricks any skater learns early on. As friends watched and cheered from the platform, leaning palms on trucks, intent, I tried to mimic the moves I'd seen in magazines, especially in *Thrasher* and *TransWorld Skateboarding*. At the very least we each rode boards by pros with whom we identified. For me it was always a Steve Caballero deck with Independent trucks and Rat Bones wheels. As we swung like pendulums from one curved side to the next, our wheels whirred beneath us, pausing if we caught air and resuming once we landed.

Our skate session didn't last long. One apparent problem with the ramp, aside from the tight transitions and lack of flat bottom, was the fact that it only had a single layer of sheeting. Our wheels began to whine over the space between two-by-fours. The structure felt rigid, but tenuous, and as each of us fakied our way up and down, pumping our legs to thrust through the transitions, hands on our oversized kneepads, the hollow sound must have clued each of us in. Our excitement started to diminish with each trick. Then someone popped a sizable air.

Over the coping his knees bent as he pulled a slight backside method. *Yeah*, we said together, in a chorus, cheering. *Yeah*. When he came down, his front wheel dug into the thin plywood sheet. It planted there with a snap in the wood, and the sight of it left a divot in our stomachs. Then there was the delayed thump of a body hitting the bottom and curling up as if holding onto the pain. For just a small second.

The Painting

There were times when I was never sure when she slept. I could walk into the house, and she would be sitting up in her wheelchair, the TV on, dozing to the theme music of a game show. Then a look on her face, her unruly eyebrows arched when she would throw her head back suddenly, as if coming to and startled to find me there. She gazed at me as I walked into the house.

In the kitchen I would find our mother trying to make dinner while our younger brothers chased each other around the wheelchair. They squealed, which sometimes caused our sister's body to jolt, but more often than not, it made her smile. Her teeth glazed with a slight drool.

What is it? I would say.

Nothing, she said with her eyes.

Though she was only five years older than me, she appeared as something ancient and delicate. Like a work of art in some museum, a painting you shouldn't touch. In the living room there was an empty space that once held a framed oil painting. The painting was from Naples, a scene of its moonlit bay and surrounding buildings. The illuminated windows of each in deep orange and reds, as if flames might burst at any moment and consume each home, piece by piece. The water, however, was the exact opposite. With its rich shades of aquamarine, it was ethereal. More lunar, more so the cosmos it reflected.

This painting our father had brought back after one of his Med cruises with the navy. Now the painting was gone from the house. Just like our father, who had left well before our sister's accident. When I looked at the blank wall, I still saw the painting. It was the same with her. I could find myself staring at Rica, her wide pupil slightly off track, her hair crazed with inattention, and yet, she could become who she had been — the beautiful one, the one who put others at ease. It wasn't just with me, either.

I didn't know when her friend Ronnie first came to visit her, only that my sister seemed happier by it, maybe the happiest she would ever be. Ronnie was Rica's age, or close to it. They had gone to middle school together, and from what I gathered, Rica had been a friend, perhaps someone who had treated him kindly when the rest of the world wouldn't. With a tall, gawky frame, Ronnie didn't possess the same physical build as the muscular football players Rica had dated in high school. Ronnie, in tucked-in faded flannel and jeans, wasn't striking, wasn't as handsome really. He drove a rusty Ford pickup truck with white mag rims. Half of the truck's body was a primer gray. But what the truck lacked in appearance, it made up for with a powerful engine, a heart that tore through silence.

He told us he was the son of a NASCAR driver, though a lesser-known one. Other than that, Ronnie didn't let on he knew a lot about engines and racing. His shyness was such that he didn't reveal a lot about himself. Not at first, at least. As for his actions, however, he began visiting Rica shortly after she had been brought home from the hospital. He would sit next to her in our living room and just listen as she tried to say words that were only clipped breaths.

He was a patient person, and his shyness only complemented his patience. We quickly learned that he was like us, hopeful. He stared at her with an expectant gaze reserved for nothing less than an intense faith. As if he knew she would just start talking to him one day, as if he wanted to be ready for what she would say when she would actually be able to say it.

I would come home from school and see his truck in front of the house, his bony elbow resting on the driver's side window rolled down most of the way. Rica would be in the passenger's seat of our car, her body favoring the side closest to the window where he would greet her by tapping on the glass, laughing like we were all trapped in a fish tank and he wasn't. I quickly realized the show was always for her, his sticking out his tongue and playfully tapping out a rhythm to get her attention, and my sister responded each time with a smirk, like she had his number. Like she knew him. Like they were already an old couple used to each other's quirks.

Waiting for Sentences

She would spell out words. Slowly. This is how we would wait for sentences to emerge. Implicating the world in which she could no longer speak. You could watch a letter form and then look out the window and hear other kids from the neighborhood riding by on bicycles, calling for you to play a game of Smear the Queer. And when you looked back at her hand, it would only then be shifting into the next vowel or consonant, and you would have to keep track of such tedium by saying the letter aloud but thinking of something else just to keep your sanity. Once she finally finished, she would look at you with a half smile, like a child, waiting for you to process what had already lived a while in her head.

Sometimes what she only wanted to mention was a small joke, maybe something she overheard on the TV, but by the time you put it all together, the humor was lost. This delay had come to define her life. As time went on, she must have sensed this, because she would only answer in one or two words, little moments for her fingers in the grand scheme of things.

But life was one long delay, wasn't it?

Things that would have been fun to enjoy were put on hold. Even the simplest tasks, ones that any average person could expect to fulfill in a given day, they quickly became milestones on an invisible chart, goals to work toward only after years of rehabilitation: washing your face, brushing your teeth, all by yourself.

Then, walking and talking. If she was lucky, she might one day have the chance to push herself up, out of her wheelchair, and cross the room. I think many in our family secretly harbored the fantasy that we could be the ones present on the day this miracle would occur. So we waited. How wonderful it would be to report conditions on the thing we collectively wanted the most. Never mind the burdens that loomed, the ones she would have to overcome alongside the minor burdens for the one reporting every detail. Even so, I used to dream of being in this situation: how to describe her eyes each time she took a step and realized no one was holding her? How to accurately record the renewal of hope within those of us who'd questioned whether or not it would ever reappear?

Once, when our mother had taken our brothers to the grocery store with her, I sat alone in the house with Rica. She was lying in bed and just staring at the door when I opened it and found her that way. How long had she been there? Why hadn't I come to her sooner? She tried to say my name, even from the doorway I could hear it, and I thought, too, that others could say my name, but my name was also the way she said it, just a breath, which is all a name really is anyway.

I sat next to the bed and stared at the way her eyes could smile. Below her chin rested the scar from her tracheotomy. In looking back, I think of a poem by William Matthew's, a simile for his navel, the *bubble* in a carpenter's level. In some ways, my sister's scar was just that, a thing to gaze upon until something within you could right itself and you would have the resolve then to look hard on her face or listen to her as she tried to say something as simple as your name.

Buh, she said. It was always this word.

I know, I said.

Buh, she said.

Yes, I said.

What do you want to be when you grow up? she said.

I think a doctor, I said. It was true. I wanted to be a surgeon. I wanted to make things right in people.

But not for me, she said.

I know, I said. You'll be fine before then.

No, it will be too late, she said.

Don't say that, I said.

It will, she said.

Whatever, I said.

Don't say whatever, she said.

Okay, I said.

So what do you want to be? she said.

I leaned closer to her and spoke my answer into the scar on her throat, as if it were a microphone meant to record everything I would ever say to her and everything after.

Short Life

The frame was a lemon yellow glaze, like you could sink your teeth into it if you wanted. It's how many coats he'd put on. Everything about the go-kart had been rebuilt. One Sunday I went with Ronnie to watch him race it at Langley Speedway. Others, equally obsessed, brought their go-karts to the track, and for a moment the world became only bright colors swirling into an oval. Those not racing watched from the infield. We clenched our fists and yelled when someone gained in lead or fell back. We clenched no matter what.

So long as these tiny engines kept whining, crescendos into decrescendo, we wouldn't have to go back to our lives. Ones I suspected most of us lived to reach these kinds of stalled moments, weekends. I don't remember if Ronnie won that day; I don't think he did, but I do remember his face after the race. Smeared in spots with smoke, he was smiling, boastful almost, though he was not a person who would be comfortable thinking others might have seen him that way.

He seemed extremely proud of himself, or maybe it was his pride for the way his go-kart performed. I know he had airbrushed my sister's name on a license plate that he'd bolted to that yellow frame. Though he didn't say it, I knew he thought of her finishing the race with him. Maybe that's why he had taken such measures, I don't know.

I thought of my sister's name being carried along the track; over and again, it swirled around me and the others who only watched with clenched fists, unaware. Some of the engines drew flames, fluttering, and then cast veils of white smoke until the drivers brought them in for a pit stop. But Ronnie had continued on with my sister's name alongside him.

After the race, I ran a finger over the pieces of gravel pressed into the melted rubber of each tire. I didn't realize how fragile the parts of a go-kart could be. Ronnie nodded and told me about the tires and their short life in a race. It made me think of other things, but I didn't say it.

On the drive back we crossed the Hampton Roads Bridge Tunnel. There was the end of the James and sailboats and the commercial fishing boats at Phoebus, near the tiny bridge entrance of Fort Monroe. The drawn arms of those boats gave them the appearance of being both alien and prehistoric, like each were mechanical pterodactyls waiting for an opportunity to resume flight. I remember glimpsing the gray fleet silhouetted to my right, the numerous piers of NOB, the naval operations base, housing the ghosts of when my sisters and I stood there next to our mother.

The giant smoke-colored ship would be pulling into port, actually gliding slowly from the dwarfed red and black tugs nudging it. We didn't know our father would be coming back from deployment with a mustache. I didn't recognize him at first, but then did, the familiar scent of Paco Rabonne. It is one of the few memories I have of my mother smiling in his presence. Both Tinah and Rica flanked his sides, drawn to him like a pair of wings. Looking back, I wonder how many times he has had to live as someone else. Whether by his own doing or not.

My father with bags packed drops them into our brushed blue late '60s Ford sedan, a Fairlane, I think it was, and we are all smiling now. We are teasing him, telling him to shave it, because we didn't have the words yet to say it simply: *Come back to us.*

IV.

Silver Plastic Suit

By the time I moved up to junior varsity, I had learned the value of the silver plastic suit. You would wear it under your sweats, and the idea was that its lack of ventilation, only a small reinforced hole at each underarm, would trap the heat around the rest of your body, forming a mobile sauna of sorts. If you ran with this suit on, especially in the heat, you could feel your will weaken a little as your skin tightened around muscles more defined by the stress. For those of us wanting to lose weight, it was an unsettling addiction, like a caustic lover, the way it took more than it gave back. There was never replenishment in the exchange.

One morning in December of my ninth-grade year, I woke at five and slid the hard plastic suit on, wrapped the rest of myself with sweats, taping at the ankles and the wrists with a cloth roll we'd kept with my sister's medical supplies. The plastic pressed into my skin, and I winced, though I knew it would soften once I got going. The rest of the house slept.

My running shoes, the front soles thin, sounded like sandpaper as they scuffed the tarmac before I found my stride through the watery, lamp-lit landscape of early morning. The light on the city water tower looming over the neighborhood continued to blink, flashing red. I rounded the corner onto Kempsville Road, and pretending an opponent was shooting in with a single leg, I sprinted counting *one-one thousand, two-one thousand* until I reached thirty and fell into the slow rhythm of a jog.

To my left the marshland hugging the curve of Battlefield Boulevard was starting to warm with first light. There was the fence of cord grass and the occasional heron. There was the spread of wetland vanishing into the various compositions of shadows. I had not yet learned to read such language, and no sooner had I finished counting to thirty, the voice in my head became the distortion in a medley of skate rock songs — Suicidal Tendencies, Black Flag, The Faction.

I could burn my heart out thinking of these anthems for anger.

Picking up speed I neared the old bridge, all silver spray and mushroom-sized rivets. There were cars passing me by as I crossed the bridge into Great Bridge proper, a sleepy coastal town that was quickly becoming a bedroom community among the seven cities yet to be named Hampton Roads. This was still Tidewater.

I left the boats tied to the docks behind me. If I concentrated I could add the small slaps of woven rope against the sides of their slick hulls. I could add the random gull complaining to the robins and catbirds swooping near the trash can at the entrance of Lock Park. I could add the raccoon on the side of the road, a bag of fur gone to the big sleep. But the only sounds that stayed with me were the distorted guitar riffs, the hollow crunch and bite of dissonance. Of overdrive, someone's RAT pedal blaring back and forth from the pickups facing an amplifier.

I had a guitar at home. A sunburst Les Paul copy my mother had taken me to a pawnshop in Norfolk to buy for fifty bucks. I loved this guitar, even though some of the wiring needed to be re-soldered, fixed. In some ways, it was no different than me. It had one setting — *annoying*, which is what I loved most about it.

Never mind that I couldn't play a lick. It didn't stop me from plugging into an old tube amp and kicking a reverb box so there would be a quick crash, a full scream of feedback. I loved to break apart the silence in my room, in this house. And I listened to anything. All forms of Elvis (Costello would come later), mainstream '80s bands, and of course skate rock and hardcore. Times when my mother would take Rica to an appointment and my brothers were in the backyard playing, sometimes working through their own anger, I would close the windows in my room and turn the volume up on my amplifier until the knob threatened to strip. The music would be crackling from the blown speakers of my boom box, and then I would destroy it.

I passed the 7-11 and the adjacent strip of shops housing Dutch Maid Donuts, where I could see one of the workers, a woman with her hair pulled back in a bun, placing a tray of sugar-dusted donuts on display. There would be time for that, I thought, but not now.

Now I had to cross the intersection at Johnstown Road and think only of the same opponent smiling gap-toothed as he shoots in again, which sends me sprinting. I throw a front headlock and dig my right shoulder against his, clamping until he pauses, and then I spin until I am behind him and the referee throws two fingers in the air.

Takedown.

I make it to the stadium behind the junior high. It is the same place where a few years before I watched Rica cheer in front of a crowd. Those were cold nights mostly, when we yelled back in response, our words formed clouds before vanishing.

I round the gravel track. No words play in my head. No guitar riffs. No distortion. When I begin my first ascent up the stadium stairs, I don't even hear the thrumming of my steps on the ribbed metal bleacher seating. I don't hear them ring, because they don't ring. I can feel the sweat gathering above my ankles, around my wrists, too, from where the suit and the sweats are cinched with cloth tape. No songs play in my head. It's quiet here, where I'm disappearing.

The Idea of Weight

It becomes the air that follows all food into my throat. It becomes the long morning run I dread before I start. It becomes the late evening practice. Whatever it is, it is always the moment of first learning there was ever an accident. Then the bending of each life afterward, to fit into every moment.

The idea of weight.

Whatever it wants it gets. My sister on me now. I'm thirteen again. I'm fourteen. Fifteen. My loose arms slipping under hers. Move forward and then adjust, inevitably counter. For these moments, we appear to be dancing.

No, not dancing. There is nothing graceful in what I attempt, nor in what her body allows. Our mother is there between us. She coaches us both with a soft voice, a hand nearby to aid if we begin to fall.

Then, my footing shifts. It is faster and less patient. I'm annoyed by my sister's lack of progress. I think, if I'm annoyed, then I've accepted her new life, her crippled self. I look for patience in the strangest places. I look into the eyes of my younger brothers. They have known her mostly as this person who must rely on even them.

She is not broken.

We are the ones who are broken.

I step in to regain my balance. I almost leap backward. I breathe. Rica, I say, help me.

She smiles.

Put your foot down, I say. She looks like a swimmer testing the water's surface with a toe. I want her to do anything other than smile and tap the ground with a crooked foot.

Rica, I say, but she pretends not to hear me. She is smiling, and I know she can tell that I'm more than a little frustrated by the lesson. I turn as if I might hip toss her into the wheelchair. I step farther inward. It takes the weight off of her crooked foot, the one trying to twist toward her. Her body is turning against us both.

It is only because this side of her body is paralyzed from the accident. I know this, but even so, I begin to think, No more Russians. No more cartwheels in the back yard. The sky blue water tower will fade into the sky without her.

I look up and stare into the brutal pupil.

It is the one that will remain forever dilated. A wide black dot. A mouth. Yes, how it resembles a mouth. Open and locked in a scream, slightly widening at the edges. I have read that black holes are formed after supernovas implode. I consider an open mouth to be a black hole in miniature. In this way there are traces of the cosmos within a subtle moment.

I think, Consider the darkness. It rests on the eye and never completely vanishes. What you see first will always be tinged.

I wonder if it has affected her, but of course, it has. And everyone we know. I'm tired of being the brother of the girl who survived the accident. What I wouldn't give to remove myself from this duty. If I could forget about her, then she would be gone entirely. All that I see seems weighted with the burden of survival. Held within your own body, and being able to do nothing about it.

She simply exists without our knowing. It weighs on everyone. Our mother says, What are you doing?

I'm still holding her up. Her legs have started shaking.

Rica, our mother says, sit down.

Rica looks at us and smiles. Buh, she says, *fuh*. She smiles wider, like it's one of the funniest things she's heard in a long time. We know she means, Fuck. We all laugh.

All images — *open mouth, black hole, brutal pupil* — they are one and the same. Since from this mouth my sister's voice has disappeared. The memory of her voice is an album of sound I've been searching through and yet slowly forgetting with each day. It is the sound, I tell myself, I must not forget. But it continues to elude me. It is something she has learned to live without. It is something we all must do at some point. Still the older sister, she instructs me by what she can no longer do.

When I look into her eye again, I'm freshly startled. How to accept what cannot be fully accepted? Her weight is tireless in the various forms it takes. I've set her down wrong. She is sliding now. I must move my arms to get a better grip. I help her back up so she can sit with her back flush to the flimsy rubber backing. I move my arms again. They are like eels in undersea crags. My hands snap at nothing, no divers shining light into the dark. I only grab hold of the loose flesh under each arm. When I feel my hands slipping again, I panic and say, Jesus *H.* Christ.

Our mother frowns.

I don't even have to look at her. I can feel the frown behind me. But again, a wide grin breaks across Rica's face. She is a joker now. It takes getting used to, yet it lets me know that some part of her is still in there. At first this is a comfort for me, as well as for the rest of the family. How many times have friends stopped by the house, eager to see any progress, any change? Though she is no longer the energetic teenager. No longer the pretty high school cheerleader, as most remember her. She changes without changing at all.

It is not until she goes on living years after the accident that the idea of her within this body becomes almost unbearable. I want to ask her so many questions. But all of her responses will be short answers. Spelled out in sign language. I'm impatient. Sometimes I ask, and sometimes I just sit there and stare into space with her. It frustrates me, and I'm left with guilt for feeling frustrated. I will watch her one hand bend fingers into each letter.

When she tries to sign, I sometimes say, *I don't know what you're saying.* She will try to sign when one of us is moving her from the car to the wheelchair or the wheelchair to the bed or from the bed to the wheelchair to the car. I'll need to concentrate on keeping her upright. I do this because I must learn how to help our mother with the burden.

Yes, Rica says.

I don't know what you're saying, I say again.

Yes, you do, she continues.

Our mother steps in and helps me. We slowly lower Rica into the wheelchair. We fold down the foot plates and, lifting each leg, guide her feet onto them. Her crooked foot never stays completely still. It taps, like she's nervous, unsure of our intentions. These people that hover around her like drones.

Once she is securely fastened, I push forward on the brake levers. Greased at the hinges, they release languidly, as if even the surrounding objects have begun to take on her physical traits. I take notice of the trace of indentations on the thick, gray rubber. The indentations look like notches in the stock of a rifle our Uncle James had shown me how to mark with a pocketknife. But that was years ago, on the family farm down near Roper. A field of new corn swaying before us.

Weight becomes the way one takes a deep breath and holds it. The way one believes that pushing anyone in a wheelchair will bring about some form of grace. Then the churning momentum, getting her over the sidewalk and to the small wooden ramp that leads inside the house of our shared childhood.

Here's the thing.

Anyone in their right mind should see a wheelchair and lavish it with irreverence, become for a moment those perfectly healthy kids that sit in wheelchairs and race each other down hospital halls until someone tells them to stop, admonishing them with looks. The wheelchair is functional this way. It allows for various translations of joy. Just not in this house. In this house the wheelchair carries more than a body. It carries the intangibles that leave the family awash in confusion.

To say it carries both angel and demon simultaneously is not quite right.

Dog

Our mother just brought him home one day, as if he were a dog. She had met him at one of the places she liked to go for drinks on nights when she needed to simply get away and forget she had daughters and sons who needed her. So much of her life had been about taking care of others, but sadly, it was at the most inopportune time that she chose to feel entitled.

The man was hardly a man. I realized early on that he was no different than those younger men one would see around the malls in Norfolk or Virginia Beach. *Squids*. Sailors who had left their homes, still in want of a mother, still angry with fathers who'd kicked them out. He had a child's gripe with the world, and at the time, I remember feeling contempt for her decision, both in choosing this man and for letting him move into the house.

It happened that one night, after he came back from work, he was sitting in the living room drinking Bud and watching TV, my brothers running around the room and causing the general ruckus that young boys have a long history of doing. He yelled at them, and they went outside. He followed them out there, only to find that they were both peeing near the pile of scrap wood he kept in the back. That's when they ran into the house screaming my name. I stood up and let them hide behind me. He rushed headlong and stopped short of thrashing us all.

Don't *touch* them, I said quietly.

Shit, he said, towering over me. Those little shits were taking
a piss outside, in front of everyone.

So, I said. *You're not touching them.* You could see the anger in
his dark eyes, soulless dots like a shark's eyes. I knew he would
hurt me, but I also knew that if he touched one of my brothers, I
would find my way into the kitchen. At some point, maybe not
that night, but one soon, and I would take a knife and slide the
blade like a cock into his mouth.

For the next year I would find my voice gone from me. I would
walk into the house, and my voice would wait for me outside. I
became silent, like my sister hours away in a rehabilitation center.
If he was in the kitchen, I was in the living room. If he went into
the living room, I went into my bedroom. I didn't speak to him
and would not speak to him. As a result, though, I felt confined. I
was still wrestling for my school, having won some junior varsity
tournaments, but I wasn't growing like my friends. I was stunted,
barely ninety pounds, if not lighter, and I was nowhere near breaking the five-foot mark in height.

Our mother was still trying to balance working nights at a con-
venience store and visiting Rica. Sometimes, my brothers played
in the aisles of that store during her shift; other times, they stayed
with me, or if I had something for school, then Tinah would come
over and watch them. There was no set schedule.

We had a dog named Duchess, a female mix with the body of a
German Shepherd, but smaller, and with a few markings of one as
well, a black muzzle that vanished into the beige fur of her head. I
remember one night our mother had come home during a break
from work, and he was outside with the dog. You could hear him
calling the dog and then getting angry when the dog didn't come
to him. I looked out the window to see him kicking Duchess. It
was her yelp that had finally made me look. Our mother heard
it too and ran outside. There was quiet for a moment, but soon,
he came back into the house. He brought with him the anger he

still had for the dog and now the anger he had for my mother and for me because I had gotten up from the table and stood between them. I smelled the stale breath of a man who was not a man at all. I smelled the stale warm breath of a thing that I should have considered alive but that I could not consider alive.

And I'm sick of you too, he said, looking away from my mother and pushing me back into the chair. He said, C'mon, you want your ass beat?

I just stared ahead, my eyes glazing over like a fish.

You need your fucking ass beat, he said. That's what you need. You fucking pussy. You think you're a man? You think you're a man? And he poked me in the chest, and he said it again, and instead of becoming the man that I should have become at that moment, I cowered.

Pensacola, by Way of New Orleans

I suppose I should have stayed with my mother and my brothers, but my father wanted me to visit him in New Orleans. He had moved there to be closer to his new job in Pascagoula. So after the school year was over, I took my first flight.

I remember putting on the foam-covered headphones that came with the bulky cassette recorder. I pushed the play button, and the headphones immediately buzzed with U2's "Where the Streets Have No Name." I knew Bono had written the lyrics for his humanitarian relief work in Ethiopia, but the words to the pop song took on a different meaning for me: *I want to run.*

I could feel tears welling up in my eyes as this first line looped back in my head and the plane darted off down the runway in Norfolk. Through the window I watched the world slant on its side, and, oddly enough, it all felt normal.

Before I'd left I asked our mother if she would do just one thing for me: *Make him leave.* That was it. That's all I wanted to have happen. I would be gone for ten days, and once I returned, I thought he would be gone too. I don't think she loved him so much as she needed to feel needed by him.

During my visit I didn't tell my father about this man. Instead, my father and I strolled aimlessly through the Quarter and ate beignets and talked about how, once the time came for applying to colleges, he wanted me to attend the naval academy. I shrugged through most our talks, which I'm sure pissed him off, but if he was upset with me then, he never showed it. I remember he smiled a lot during my visit, and I did the same.

As for the turmoil surrounding life back in Great Bridge, I didn't mention anything to my father really. I suppose I didn't want to expose my mother anymore than I had to. The real reason, though, was that I was embarrassed for not having stood up to this man who threatened both my mother and me. In some ways I had let both of my parents down. They had raised a boy who would not become a man.

Of course, when I returned home, I found nothing had changed. My mother pretended that we had never had an agreement. He was still in the house, and I could feel myself, after the brief reprieve, needing to force myself back into a silence I could no longer endure. It's as if I had finally been given a chance to breathe, and now someone was saying, Don't breathe, and there was no logical reason I could find that would explain why I should listen to anyone other than myself.

So, shortly after coming back home, I left again. I finally told my father, and like that, I was gone from everyone, my mother, my sisters, my brothers, my best friend John. None of them knew I was leaving for good. It was as if I had disappeared back into that ocean from a few years before, and I resurfaced to find my father holding onto me and not letting go.

I grew. I mean literally *grew*. The moment I stepped off the plane, I felt as though I started gaining weight, growing taller as well. I know this sounds crazy. I couldn't help but think my lack of growth, though, was tied to the living conditions I had recently escaped. I loved my mother and my brothers, but I hated going back to the house we all shared.

My father had made arrangements for me to stay with a family in Pensacola. It was one of his buddies from the navy, Terry, a man I remembered my father moved in with after my parents had separated years before. Terry and my father had shared a small bachelor's apartment in Ocean View in Norfolk, and now this man had a family in Pensacola, and I was lucky enough to stay there with them while my father had to go out of town for awhile on business. I had left my family in one state to go live with strangers in another state.

Despite the irony I was thankful. This family, which included two young children and their mother, I still remember fondly. They lived among other Filipino families in Pensacola. That summer I was given a chance to pretend.

The neighborhood was new, with bright homes lining the smooth tarmac of the new street. I would mow the grass for them, but that was the extent of any semblance of responsibility. If I wanted to get up and go outside, I didn't have to wonder where my brothers were. I could spend the rest of the day simply riding my skateboard up and down those streets. I could go as fast as I wanted to and as far.

On weekends we would spend evenings with other Filipino families, and it was there, at one of the gatherings, that I met a girl. She was older, getting ready to start her freshman year at college. I remember I dyed my hair that summer and started spiking it up. I must have looked out of place to her, among the other boys that were darker, with coarse black hair and the features that come with being pure, not mixed like me. I could be someone else here, and I was. I wasn't the boy who had a sister in a wheelchair. I was someone else. I wasn't the boy who had to live in a house with a man who hated him.

I was someone else.

It wasn't long before this girl and I started spending time together, going to the local mall, doing a lot of nothing and thinking we were doing something. I remember the first time I went into her house. Her mother was cooking fish, and the air smelled like my ninang's house, the warm scent of garlic and oil. There was the signature plastic-covered furniture with which many Filipinos decorated their living rooms.

You left your shoes or sandals at the door, and you came into the house and said hello to her family, even though her father wouldn't look at you. Later, you would learn it was because he wanted her to date someone full Filipino, not mestizo. But that was fine with you, because you were someone else. You told yourself that, when he didn't shake your hand.

Not too long afterward you would be alone with her where you were still staying, and the square wrapper, even with perforated edges, would slip out of your hands like a minnow. You would laugh, and she would laugh. You would try again to rip it open. This time with success, but it would be short-lived. You take out what's inside the wrapper and have trouble unrolling it.

In all of those talks, years before in the fort under the clouds of smoke and the thunder of coughing, never did you consider how you would figure into the moment, especially once you were faced with the moment itself. You had forgotten to put it to the tip first and then roll it downward. You try to widen the rubbery ring with your fingers and shove yourself in.

When she asks, *What are you doing?* You turn and face her, frustrated, the thing dangling from your finger.

What the hell? she says, and you both laugh again.

I know, you say, though you don't have a clue.

You toss that one to the side and open another, studying it for a second.

Then you do.

Promises

Not long after that, my father married again. He had been dating a woman I had met before, who lived in Mobile, Alabama. Mobile was less than an hour from where I was staying in Pensacola. He called to tell me he was coming to pick me up, that I was going to live with Liz until he was done with some obligations at work. Which meant, again, I wouldn't be living with him exactly.

It hadn't been the best timing by any means, my arrival back into his life. Over the phone I wanted to tell him what had happened with this girl, as if my father would pat me on the back once he saw me in person. No sooner had we finished talking than he was there to move me to Mobile. It happened so quickly. I only remember sharing a tearful goodbye with this family that had taken me in. That was all. Though I was normally fine in moments of unknowing, I felt crushed by what I couldn't control in my life.

The drive to Mobile was a quiet one. Crossing the long I-40 stretch that bridged Mobile Bay, we said little to each other. I felt my father was somehow disappointed in me, as if he knew. *I don't want you to see that girl anymore*, he said out of the blue. *Do you understand?* I didn't tell him that I had her phone number and her address at the new dorm on a piece of paper in my front pocket. I was going to contact her first chance I had, whether he wanted me to or not.

What do you mean? I said.

That girl is trouble, he said. I was stunned. How could he even think that about her? He didn't even know her.

She's really not, I said.

You'll find a nice girl, he continued, don't worry.

It turns out some of his own worry had to do with the fact that he didn't want me to date a Filipina. But there were other reasons unexplained to me. I looked at the lights coming on in the city ahead. This girl and I would speak on the phone a few times. We would tell each other things I have since forgotten, that we would write one another.

But we would not write one another. Though I didn't wish to be that person, I would make promises I couldn't keep.

Everything and Nothing

In Mobile I would be alone again.

I'd found I liked being alone. Liz worked at an office job, and though I enjoyed her company in the evenings, I also enjoyed the range of freedom I had throughout the day. After she would leave for work, I would explore the city.

I took my skateboard in search of new spots to grind or launch airs from or just bust my ass. I quickly met other skate punks that shared a passion for the widely known motto *Skate and Destroy*! But we weren't vagrants in the way the people gawking at us thought we were. We just wanted to shred, which was another way of saying we wanted everything and nothing at the same time.

Our afternoons revolved around hitting the tried-and-true areas along Government Street, places where there were overly-painted curbs perfect for rail sliding or forcing fifty-fifties or just popping ollies over. One of the kids had a ragged quarter pipe. Shoving our boards underneath it, we'd scoot the bulky wooden structure around town. We placed it in abandoned parking lots where we could launch hippy twists or one footers or big foots. Other times we'd set it flush against the back of a building, and getting lots of speed going, we'd whip our momentum up onto the slick vertical and thrust swathes of power slides, our coned wheels smearing screeches in unison.

If we weren't on Government Street, we were on Airline. If we weren't on Airline, we were skating a spot we nicknamed Graveyard. Graveyard was a worn series of graffitied ditches that curved near the perimeter of a cemetery.

Government, Airline, Graveyard.

Government, Airline, Graveyard.

One after the other, each spot was like a cog that spun slowly into the next, and we moved this way through the ritual of burning through the last of the summer's days.

A few weeks later I was enrolled in the local high school. It was my junior year, and instead of getting ready for the Ring Dance back in Great Bridge, I was a good fifteen hours away by car, learning the pep rally songs in support of the Murphy High Panthers. Murphy had no wrestling team, something that left me a little depressed, especially since I had been undergoing a serious growth spurt. I had gained nearly twenty pounds in the last two months alone. I felt stronger. I felt like I was truly becoming someone else, like I could rip somebody's head apart. I didn't want to stop growing, even if this phase in my life was physically excruciating. At nights, I would lie in bed and feel my joints ache, turn hollow and burn. Someone was trying to start a fire inside me.

The room I stayed in at Liz's house was a spare one filled with things, one being an acoustic guitar that belonged to her daughter Deborah. Deborah and I hit it off the first time we met. Some nights it would just be us sitting in the living room talking. She would ask me about my mother and about Rica and the rest of the family. I could talk easily with her. In many ways she reminded me of Rica. Afterward, I would usually go back to my room and pick up the guitar and just start playing.

Aside from skateboarding, music was a passion of mine that I felt I had to cultivate. At first it was because I wanted to finally learn how to play. Back then you could learn three chords and

figure out the basic structure of songs by popular bands such as
The Smiths, REM, and U2. I also couldn't leave out the sustenance
I'd drawn from the dissonance of Suicidal Tendencies, Circle Jerks,
and Angry Samoans.

So I found a chord book. I practiced the odd fingerings. I also
found I could play by ear. The inevitable calluses began forming on my fingertips. It was a rite of passage, one I knew would
sustain me.

I had made some friends at Murphy. We would go out to field
parties and stand by the whining generators while local bands jarred
the darkness, until the cherry red lights of the police popped brightly
and sent us scattering. We even formed a band of our own and called
ourselves Queen Mary Goes Down. Of course, being teenagers, we
liked telling people our name, especially the girls in our classes.

What does that mean? they would ask.

What do you think it means? we would ask in response, smirking.

Our singer wore all black and had long flaming red hair that
hung down past her waist. She would wail more than she would
actually sing, and the song lyrics were always from the poems she
had written in her journal. I didn't know anything about poetry,
except that I liked the way the language seemed to house a music
all its own.

As for the meaning in many poems I'd read, including our singer's, I couldn't care less. I wasn't a poet. I just liked making chords
with my fingers. Mashing sloppy bar chords mostly. The awkward
placements made me think immediately of sign language.

I'd strum and hear the notes blend into an existence.

I'd strum, and one night would blur into the next.

To say I was finally having fun as a sixteen-year-old was probably as close to the truth as I would have been able to muster. It
was more than fun. It was distraction from everything I had lived
up to that moment.

I wasn't especially comfortable thinking about what made me happy, but I found this break a welcome one. I would go out with Danny, who played lead guitar in Queen Mary Goes Down, and we would hang at the Four Strong Winds coffeehouse. It was just a painted cinderblock building, what appeared to be a renovated gas station. All the skate punk kids would lounge and glower in the corners sipping hot cider or tea or coffee. It was the scene, and for a brief moment in my life, I felt I was part of the scene. It was easy. All I had to do was pretend not to care.

There was a small stage in a side room, and a crowd of regulars packed the tables nearby and clapped for their friends. We had played a gig at a downtown loft owned by one of the well-known Indie bands in Mobile. Though I'm sure our guitars were out of tune and we rushed our set, there was a certain thrill that came with performing. I remember staring up from my random strumming and gazing into eyes glowing from the black light, little pinpricks in the cloth of night.

Just in Case

Shortly after the gig, I had to go back to Virginia for my custody hearing. I was a son who had to sit in a shadowy room and tell a family court judge why I wanted to live with my father and not my mother. The real truth was I didn't know what I really wanted. In the courtroom I looked out at the different people, those strangers listening to the details of our lives. I didn't care. I told myself I didn't care.

I told myself that as soon as we were through with this display, I could forget everything that had happened to me and return to Mobile and start over. I was ready to all but disappear in my thinking when the varsity wrestling coach showed up. He had come to the courthouse to see me. My mother must have called him, and at first I was pissed she would resort to such manipulation. Despite my initial anger it was a relief to find a familiar face among so many strangers. Then I remembered feeling my breathing begin to race, my voice breaking as I tried to speak to this man who had taught me, along with my teammates, the value of endurance.

Moments before, I had stepped out of the judge's chambers, nearly crying from when I'd told the judge how I never wanted to live with my mother again. I wanted to punish her, I wanted to punish myself. I remained silent. The man peered at me over his bifocals. He stared a long time before he finally spoke. I think he could see something that I had not yet realized.

I tell you what, he said. I'm going to give you some more time to think about this. Just in case.

Just in case what? I said.

Just in case you change your mind, son.

The day before I left for Mobile, I had the chance to see Rica again, but just briefly. She kept touching my face and patting my head. She was smiling, asking me where I had been. I didn't know what to tell her. I asked her if she liked my hair. I had tried over and again to dye it, to lighten it to the same blonde color as my favorite skater Steve Caballero's, but I didn't use the right products. My hair had turned mostly orange. It was ridiculous, spiked high in a defiant consolation.

That night I stayed with my sister Tinah. She was living with friends in an apartment directly across the street from my old junior high school. John had come over as well, which gave us a chance to catch up. It had been nearly five months since I had seen my best friend.

When Tinah and her friends finally turned in for the night, John and I stayed up and talked about stupid shit at first. Then we found a full bottle of gin on top of the refrigerator. It wasn't long before we had opened the bottle and started taking shots. We laughed, joking about the various inane things we'd done here and there, each time portioning out the gin until the room was filled with the cleansing odor of our laughter.

At one point we had fallen to the floor, both of us on our backs and staring at the warped ceiling of my sister's apartment. We could have been in the middle of nowhere. An early morning sky above us. The air we breathed was crisp and burned in our throats.

Hey, John said.

What?

Tell me something.

I waited for him to keep going, but he didn't. There was just silence. It settled in my ears, like an almost audible pause.

When I looked over at him, I saw only the side of his face, a few tears. He said something then, but I didn't know what he said.

What?

Why did you leave? he said quietly.

He knew more than anyone why I had left, or at least, in my mind, I thought he knew more than anyone.

You know why, I said finally.

Not that, he said.

Then what?

You didn't even tell me you were going, he said. You could've at least told me.

He was right. I had left without ever telling my best friend goodbye.

Return

After my father had finished his contract work, he came to stay with us for good. By this time, though, it was also nearing Christmas. At Danny's house his mother had decorated their home with fresh pine wreaths and giant red velvet bows and holly and all kinds of ornaments. It had left every room resonant with a feeling of warmth and festivity.

I remember standing in their kitchen, not thinking of anything except the approach of the holiday, Danny joking around with his pretty older sister. She had recently come home from college. It was hypnotic, watching this brother and sister play as if they couldn't stand each other in one moment and then hugging in the next. Danny's mother would pat at the two as she moved from room to room.

That's when the call came.

Rica was dead.

V.

The Sky

I'd wanted my sister to die, until she did.

She is buried in a cemetery on Cedar Road in Great Bridge. It is the road our family for years had taken every Sunday to church. For her funeral there was a Mass at Prince of Peace, where I had been an altar boy, and Rica was there, her open coffin attended by the colorful sprawl of flower arrangements.

Inside it all, she rested. Our mother, in her grief, wanted Rica buried in her cheering uniform. I was through with being embarrassed by my sister's tragedy. I didn't care what those who'd gathered that day thought, especially of the broken girl dressed in green and gold.

During the offering, we gathered as a family and walked in a processional to the casket. I knew this would be my last chance to touch her, so I did. I kissed the cold flesh of her forehead. I felt the bumps that had been covered with makeup. I told her I was sorry, but even then, I knew it didn't matter.

Outside it started to drizzle.

The other pallbearers, my friend John among them, helped me carry her. She was heavy, surprisingly so, and there was some minor struggle placing her into the back of the hearse. At the gravesite we would walk her one more time. It felt like a greater distance than we had just traversed at the church. There could have been anything in the coffin then, chunks of pavement reassembled into a road, a piece of the car on that same road. What I remember of the graveside ceremony was the gray sky and the way the random drops of rain streaked our cheeks. I looked over and saw Ronnie, thin in his dark suit. He had helped carry her too and was now wiping his face. I was doing the same.

◑

So what happened? I asked her.

Nothing, she said. Not long after you left, he did too. He should have left long ago.

Oh, I said. I knew I had to tread lightly. So, are you doing all right?

She looked at me like I had said something funny, but she wasn't going to laugh. She smiled slowly. You do the best you can do, she said.

I could tell she was bordering on the defensive. Whether it was from her having lost someone she loved or someone she didn't love, it was the same. There was still loss involved. Rica had been her favorite. That was no secret among us.

You're right, I said. I stared up at the tin picture of *La Ultima Cena*, the Last Supper. I was convinced every Filipino family in America had one in the same place, there above the table. That, and a pair of oversized wooden utensils. The giant fork-and-spoon set.

Do you like living with Dad? she said, as if to get me to look at her.

I didn't want to say I did. I didn't want to say I had freedom there, and that I was being taken care of, that if I stayed in Mobile I could see myself living an easier life than the one I had left here in Great Bridge.

But I missed her and the rest of the family.

It's nice, I offered.

Oh, she said now and looked into her coffee cup. We were sitting in the kitchen, our reflections in the window from the night sky pressed against the other side of the glass. My brothers were sleeping in the next room. Our cat Princess came into the room, rubbed herself against my leg, and then left. She was the stray that, years before, Rica had lunged out of her wheelchair trying to grab. Rica had broken a tooth from hitting the sidewalk.

I looked around the kitchen. There were the same pots our mother had used to cook our meals. They were drying, turned upside down on a cloth towel spread on the counter. Behind me the door to the pantry stayed open. You could see inside, on one of the bottom shelves, the black speckled pot Rica had used to boil cabbage. I wondered then if everything in this house would forever remind me.

◑

By the time I got there, my mother continues, they had put her in her room, and it looked like *someone had taken a pencil and drawn a line right down the middle of her body.* I try not to picture this in my mind, but I do. The image of the halving seems poignant, but again, I try not to make the connection. My mother is talking about my sister. I am listening and not listening.

My mother adds that Rica's right side had purpled from where the blood in her body had gathered. In the story, my sister had been sitting up in her wheelchair, out in the sunroom at Lake Taylor Rehabilitation Center, and, at some point in the day, had leaned over too far and had simply stopped breathing. That's how the staff found her.

Before they transferred her to the funeral home, my parents had to drive out there to see Rica in the morgue. There were my parents in the same room. I've thought about this image over the years, that Rica would bring them together again, if only to view what it is they once had. For in my memory, even if it's purely my wanting it to be this way, they are filled with grief because a part of them remembers the day she was born to them, with her full head of black hair and her slender fingers and toes. How many times did our mother unfold Rica from the swaddling just to see her tiny legs kick, her fists bunched and punching in random, nervous jolts? I believe their grief was rooted in this first moment of her life. At the end, on the drive back, they would say things to one another they should have never said. It is understandable. But nothing, not even the resentments compiled over the course of their marriage and beyond, would last longer than the image of their daughter naked, as if she were a newborn all over again.

The Wrong Bus

When I was five years old, having just started kindergarten at B. M. Williams Primary, I got on the wrong bus. For some reason the bus that normally picked me up and dropped me off had been switched. Maybe our driver was sick, I don't know, but an announcement was made that anyone riding our bus number needed to ride another bus. Or so I thought, scrambling with my things to climb the wide-lined steps of the new bus. It wasn't until we began spiraling out of the circular bus ramp that I started looking around at the other kids. I didn't see Timmy or Hill or anyone else from my neighborhood. I should've spoken up then, but I didn't.

Instead, I sat quietly as the bus made its stops. One by one, kids left the big cushy seats and returned to their former lives. One by one, the noise of chatter grew less pronounced. When the bus made its final routine drop off, the driver looked up to see me peeking at her from the last seat, the one that braced against the emergency exit door. I felt like taking that door.

Honey, she said and motioned for me to come up to the front.

I grabbed my backpack and my tin Kung Fu lunchbox, with scenes from the television series starring David Carradine. The bus lurched, and I reached for the sides of each seat as I tried to walk the aisle, stumbling a little before I made it to the seat nearest the driver. I waited until I was close to her before I answered her, something my father always insisted I do with him. Yes, I said.

Where do you live, honey? she said.

I peered ahead through the blue-tinted window as the bus kept moving forward. I remember being almost hypnotized by the way the gray road kept diving underneath the front of the bus. We were on a road that ran alongside an empty field, one that had been harvested. Nearly blond stalks spread across the light blue dirt. They were splayed in chopped bunches. Harvesting spared nothing. I knew this from weekend visits to my mother's family's farm in North Carolina.

Then I looked beyond the tree line for the blue water tower. I searched for anything that might be familiar to me, but I found nothing. I was alone. I couldn't even say where I was from or where I should go. It was only then that my panic began to reach my throat. In a shaky voice I told this woman as much about my life as I could. I told her my name and my parents' names and the street address and my kindergarten teacher's name. I don't know how long I kept talking. I told her I had two sisters, they were older, and that they both went to Crestwood Elementary.

The bus didn't turn around, or it didn't seem to turn around. We continued along the road where the fields were all shorn. I looked at my lunchbox, at the various scenes depicting an event in Kane's new life, each one a lesson. Before long I started hearing a car horn. It could have been anything though. A flock of geese flying low perhaps. But it wasn't. We both knew, though the driver looked back at me and asked. I said, *Yes yes yes yes*, and she slowed the bus and then it stopped and the door folded open and whatever she had said then, I can't remember, because I didn't turn around to look at her.

I only had eyes for my mother.

Even as I approached the station wagon, my mother was still honking at the bus. I was smiling with relief as I dodged sprigs of grass lining the ditch. My backpack and my lunchbox swinging wildly at my side. My whole world suddenly fell back into place.

Homecoming

It wasn't long after Rica's funeral that I told my father I wanted to go back and finish at Great Bridge. He didn't understand, which is to say he was angry with me. He had gone out of his way to make accommodations. I had disrupted other lives in the shuffling and reshuffling. Yes, I was being selfish. Yes, I didn't realize what problems I had already caused and would continue to cause. I agreed with him. Not wanting to, I reaped his silence. I was a son who didn't appreciate the opportunities I had before me. I was being selfish, I know.

But I also wanted to tell him something. I was becoming a man. No one had told me to make the decision that would break my father's heart. I had come to that on my own. I knew that he was going to be fine, that he was married again, and that things were going good for him in Mobile. I was a son who felt he had a sense of duty. Even so, I couldn't say to him that I was worried about her. I couldn't say to him whatever new life he had placed before me was a consolation. He had to feel it. I felt it, had felt it when I'd talked to my mother after Rica's death. There are things you must weigh. I didn't want my life to be a consolation.

Here's what I knew: my mother's sole purpose in life had been jarred by the loss. Prior to Rica's death my mother had spent a great deal of time attending to her, even when Rica was living in various rehabilitation centers across the state. My mother had traveled great distances both physically and mentally. Not that my father hadn't, but my mother bore particular burdens in my sister's disabled life. My mother, after all, had been the one to let her go to the Outer Banks in the first place. My mother was reminded in many ways. Now, she would never let her go, as if a pact were being made with the ghost.

Despite the fact that my mother would no longer need to coordinate her schedule around what Rica needed, no longer need to keep searching for medical procedures that would allow Rica to regain some semblance of her former self, there was still the weight of her absence to figure. None of us would be prepared.

Rica left behind a roomful of clothes, both the ones she had worn before the accident and the ones she had worn afterward. In one phase of her life, there were the bright skirts and blouses, tight jeans and short shorts. Our mother would hold them up in the air and shake her head before folding them and placing them into boxes.

In the last phase of Rica's life, there were the mismatched jogging pants and sweatshirts, the ones worn until the stains could no longer be washed away. These clothes, along with the wheelchair, would be packed away to gather dust in a room of our mother's house. Then they were unpacked and then packed away again. Then they were stuffed into closets, into the attic, into another room. They seemed to move on their own. They formed a quiet wall. They vanished behind other walls of boxes, more accumulation.

After the remainder of Rica's things had been hidden from sight, there were the photographs with which one had to contend. What to keep and what to throw away became too difficult to determine, so nothing was thrown away. It was easier, if ease could at all be attributed to a memory, to a legacy of struggle that defies definition in the hearts of those who witnessed it. No hospital bills were thrown away. No legal documents wrapped in thick rubber bands were tossed as refuse.

Nothing was given away, and so nothing remained. Old flowers had been saved. Flowers from before the accident. Flowers afterward, shoved into boxes and drained of color until they became something else. Then silk flowers put on the grave. Silk petals on silk flowers sun-bleached and gathered and put back again on the same grave and then again and then new flowers and then the flowers put into a box in one of the rooms of the house and forgotten. The new flowers finally forgotten, and the room forgotten.

Always new flowers.

Ritual

The field was like a snow globe broken open, a lush untouched sheet of dandelions warmed in the sun. We had spent the day wrestling three sessions, two hours each filled with drills. Afterward, we washed the mats to prepare again for the next morning filled with repetition. It was how we learned our moves, engraving them in the brain, and by evening, after we had showered and taken in the persistent heat lingering near the hilly landscape of Farmville, we sat on the porch and tried to think of things to keep ourselves busy. Some of us had started chewing tobacco, and for a spell, we all tried. There was the peppermint scent of the chew fighting the Ben-Gay with which we had smothered our arms and legs.

After a few days we grew tired of sitting on the porches of the dorms where we stayed. The heat followed us wherever our gaze rested. More often than not it lay on the field that buffered the old buildings, the grass in patches meshed against the dandelions.

It was still early one evening when the boy was seized by the ritual, by those who seemed hypnotized by the haze of humidity and boredom. The boy was only a year younger than most of us, but those holding his arms and legs didn't care. They had hogtied him with his own T-shirt, and the boy, paler than the white tufts that scattered as they lay him down, started laughing hysterically. It is his laughter I want to remember.

Shaving cream canisters shook in the periphery, a circle of violent shaking occurring around the boy who coughed as he laughed and laughed as he shouted, Stop it, stop it, stop it, the octave of his voice growing progressively higher and more annoying in his panic. If you found him just then, you would think he was possessed. His eyes widened, and he didn't care that he spit his plea, that his breathing took in the delicate stalks breaking with every swing of his head from side to side, the milky smear on the back of his head. Stop it, stop it, stop it, he kept saying, but no one did.

Someone shoved in a sock, which forced him to swallow his own voice. That he kept laughing made everyone there want to see what would make him stop. The intent was to give him a pink belly, so the slapping began and did not cease. He struggled, and any shaving cream nearby grounded thousands of seedlings. Others lifted with grayish blades and spun like tiny helicopters into the fray of our vision. For those drenched or crushed, these weeds would die where they were. But a few would spread, find a way to survive.

When they let him go, he didn't stray. I was proud of him. I know that sounds ridiculous, but I was. He spit on the ground, there in front of each of us, and began laughing. All you guys can go *fuck yourselves*, he said. It didn't matter if we had held him or not. We nodded and patted him on the back. I'm serious, he said.

◗

If you've heard of the Granby sit-up, then you knew more than he did. You would have known not to lie down on the floor and let someone roll up a T-shirt and hold it over your eyes while you cross your arms in front of your chest and someone holds your feet. When someone says to you, All right, let's see if you can do a sit-up now, you would not have thought, This is the moment I'll show those fuckers. No, knowing what the Granby sit-up was, you would have rested your back to the cold tile and waited until they grew bored and pulled the T-shirt away.

But the boy from earlier in the field has, like all boys, something to prove. He doesn't know what's in store for him. He only knows that the T-shirt smells like sweat, and the room smells like farts, and the words, C'mon, Pussy, C'mon, Pussy, Up, Up, Up, smell like the mashed letters in canned vegetable soup. The boy's abs tighten, he laughs, blurts, Fuck this shit, and then everyone is laughing as he continues to strain to break free of what holds him back. There is nothing our pride will not exploit.

I want to tell him it's okay, you don't need to prove anything, but that would only be me now, older, and not the one holding one side of the T-shirt and quietly letting go so like a spring finally sprung, this boy's body comes flying forward with such force. He cannot stop himself from being cast face first into the moist hell of another boy's ass. Sadly, we cannot stop ourselves from laughing.

Another Homecoming

We're in the crowd. It's cold, and whatever you say finds its way into the air and stalls before vanishing entirely. Already the two teams have torn through the unrolled banners decorated by the cheerleaders, painted with spirit slogans. Already the well-wishing decorations have been obliterated and litter the shadowy end zones, where packs of high school kids straggle, their parents and the rest of this town clumped into the crumbling concrete edifice of stadium seating.

I make my way down to the sidelines, to the frozen undulant chain link that keeps the crowd off the asphalt track encircling the blistered field of halftime. Trucks begin to rev their engines, rumbling in the dark beyond the open double door gateway, and I wait to see her, but I can't make her out just yet. I can hear the girls' shrill chants peak just above the gurgling double-barrel carburetors, but that's all. The first floats fall into place and begin to move along the track in a clockwise direction. Everyone is smiling. Everyone is waving and wanting desperately to be seen waving. I know I am.

After a string of bright floats, I see her. She is sitting on the hood of a blue convertible muscle car. I don't know who's driving, but they are cautious, slowing and not crowding the trailer in front of them. Rica is all smiles, her thick green cheerleading sweatshirt beaming with a bright gold GBH stitched in the chest, her pompoms occasionally levitating in front of her, as if by magic, their core shaking at intervals, releasing the frenetic energy of this homecoming.

Rica, I yell to get her attention. I want people to know she is my sister. I want everyone to see her, and then look over at me, and say, Oh, that must be her brother. He looks just like her. I want nothing more than to be her brother in this one moment of our shared lives.

I don't remember if she sees me. I think she does. A part of me thinks she sees me and calls me by my nickname, which she would know embarrasses me in public. But that would be a minor thing, to carry that kind of embarrassment, especially from her. Just look. The car carries her, carting her out to be adored by the people of this town, and promises to deliver her once more around the track. I'm there in the crowd waiting for her to come back. More floats pass, streamers of bright crepe paper fluttering in the cold.

But I think I still see her.

Old Nags Head Road

You pass over the bridge, the Albemarle Sound behind you now. You pass the intersection that makes you cringe, the stoplights on the main road that look new.

It has been years.

Construction farther down, more stores, more cottages appearing in the distance and then bunching into the rearview mirror of your first car, a burnt orange Volvo. It sways, at times, like something rudderless, without a centerboard to keep it from drifting.

The Wright Brothers Memorial is still there, the long slope of the hill where their machinery, twin propellers and some rigging, became something else entirely. You pass Jockey's Ridge State Park, the range of sand on the sound side, and the ghosts of family vacations spent climbing it and sliding down its enormous, shifting face.

You pass by the familiar.

Something in your head had clicked off long ago. It's a comfort to know where you're going.

You park the car in a small lot on Old Nags Head Road. There are some friends' cars wedged between splattered work trucks, the beds filled with buckets of caulking tubes and hammers and such. Gulls spiral in the bright distance.

The waves are so good, the locals, construction workers mostly, have ended for the day and are out. Beyond, the sets rolling in hold up in places for those darting toward the inside sections, those negotiating the constant upheaval of the ocean.

So you take down your board and lay it in the sand. You fish through the trash on the floorboard for the last piece of Sex Wax and rub it in quick, but smooth, strokes across the top of the deck blistered with remnants of past sessions. Fresh wax over the old. The chemical scent of coconut, something faintly tropical, mixes with the cool salt air blowing in, hammering your senses. Tucking the board under your arm, you sprint into the churning water.

When you reach the first section, it pounds your head and shoves you around. It wants you to know that you don't belong here. You think you see your friends nearby, but then a wall lifts, sucking back. You duck dive, dig your arms in deep, and feel the sheets of water gather behind you, like all of this is simply a difficult thrashing, and yet, after some surfacing and more diving and then surfacing, you're a good eighty yards off shore now. The current continues to churn. Waves breaking on the outside leave a thick lather that makes the surface of the ocean appear more like a field covered in the white fluffy heads of dandelions. A place to tear through in a full-on run, covering the sky in those little parachuted seedlings.

Your friends have drifted away.

When you sit up on your board and scan the distant sets rolling in, you find them barely there, all shadows, smeared dots like floaters in your scarred field of vision. She is gone, but you have brought the brutal pupil with you.

Had you not just returned from wrestling camp, you would never have agreed to paddle out in nearly double overhead waves. They are choppy but thick, a good storm blowing in from northeast of the Outer Banks. For some, paddling out would seem suicidal. You suppose a part of you feels driven by how to tempt Fate. A few years before, you nearly drowned a handful of miles from this same beach.

You look to the outside.

There, a larger bump resembling the side of a giant whale rolls lengthwise through the distant blue field until it rises higher. It's not a whale, but what you imagine to be a whale. Or a submarine rolling downhill, at play in this field of dandelions.

No, it's just a lot of water moving mindlessly in your direction. It jacks up. It swells and flattens with a peak, like the hood of an immense cobra suddenly taking on form. You are furious, quickly paddling into position. You've come this far. The trough sucks back now, and you rise into the crest, settle just under the fangs.

You take a breath and free fall.

In the American Lives series

Secret Frequencies
A New York Education
by John Skoyles

Phantom Limb
by Janet Sternburg

Yellowstone Autumn
A Season of Discovery
in a Wondrous Land
by W. D. Wetherell

To order or obtain more information on these or other University of
Nebraska Press titles, visit www.nebraskapress.unl.edu.

Other Works by Jon Pineda

Birthmark
The Translator's Diary